Cracking the NYC
Specialized High Schools
Admissions Test
(SHSAT)

Cracking the NYC Specialized High Schools Admissions Test (SHSAT)

BY JONATHAN ARAK

2004 EDITION

RANDOM HOUSE, INC.
NEW YORK

www.PrincetonReview.com

Princeton Review Publishing
2315 Broadway
New York, NY 10024
E-mail: editorialsupport@review.com

ISBN: 978-0-375-76333-5

Editor: Ellen Mendlow
Production Editor: Maria Dente
Production Coordinator: Jennifer Arias
Illustrations by: The Production Department of The Princeton Review

Manufactured in the United States of America.

9 8 7 6

2004 Edition

CONTENTS

ACKNOWLEDGEMENTS

Thanks to the following for their contributions to this book:

Jinhee Bae, Akil Bello, John Bergdahl, Morgan Chase, Adam Cherensky, Roberto Colon, Robert Cohen, Dan Edmonds, Jon Freedman, Celeste Ganderson, Betsy Goldstein, Effie Hadjiioannou, Clayton Harding, Bob Hillman, Melissa Kavonic, Meher Khambata, Alex Kim, Jane Lacher, Sharon Laidlaw, Erica-Lee Lewis, Naomi Levy, Khalida Lockheed, Nava Lubelski, Charles Mastin, Paul Maniscalco, Mindy Myers, Chee Pae, John Pak, Jill Pearson, Victoria Printz, Carmine Raspaolo, James Rubin, Lisa Ruyter, Longhair Thomas, Shao-Bai Wu, Jeannie Yoon, Kelsey, Ted and Oliver, and the staff and students of The Princeton Review.

Special thanks to Adam Robinson, who conceived of and perfected the Joe Bloggs approach to standardized testing, and many of the other techniques in this book.

PROFILES OF THE SPECIALIZED HIGH SCHOOLS

Students must take the SHSAT exam at an assigned site, determined on the basis of where they have attended school.

Bronx: The Bronx High School of Science

Brooklyn: Except Community School Districts 13, 14, and 15, Brooklyn Technical High School

Queens: Long Island City High School

Manhattan, Staten Island, and Community Schools Districts 13, 14, and 15: Stuyvesant High School

These locations are subject to change. Go to **schools.nyc.gov** to confirm the latest test locations.

TEST DATES FOR 2008

Eighth grade: Last weekend in October
Ninth grade: First weekend in November

BRONX HIGH SCHOOL OF SCIENCE

75 West 205th Street
Bronx, New York 10468
School: (718) 817-7700
Admissions: (718) 295-0200 ext. 497
Fax: (718) 733-7951
Website: www.bxscience.edu

Number of Students: 2,700

Languages: French, Spanish, Russian, Italian, Chinese, Japanese, Modern Greek, Hebrew, German

BROOKLYN TECHNICAL HIGH SCHOOL

South Elliot Place at DeKalb Avenue
Brooklyn, New York 11217
School: (718) 858-5150
Admissions: (718) 858-5150, ext. 475
Fax: (718) 260-9245
Website: www.bths.edu

Number of Students: 4,600

Languages: French, Italian, Spanish

STUYVESANT HIGH SCHOOL

345 Chambers Street
New York, New York 10282-1099
School: (212) 312-4800
Admissions: (212) 312-4800 ext. 1013
Fax: (212) 587-3874
Website: www.bths.edu

Number of Students: 3,000

Languages: French, German, Hebrew, Latin, Spanish, Italian, Japanese, Chinese

For additional information on the science high schools and Summer Discovery Program, as well as two complete practice SHSAT tests, you can get a copy of the *Specialized High Schools Student Handbook* from your guidance counselor or, by written request, from the Office of High School Admissions, 22 East 28th Street, New York, NY 10016.

HIGH SCHOOL FOR MATH, SCIENCE AND ENGINEERING AT CITY COLLEGE

138th Street and Convent Avenue
New York, New York 10031
School: (212) 220-8179
Admissions: (212) 220-8179
Fax (212) 220-8204

Number of Students: 500

Languages: Beginning German, Advanced Spanish, with other languages to be added.

HIGH SCHOOL OF AMERICAN STUDIES AT LEHMAN COLLEGE

Bedford Park Boulevard West
Bronx, New York 10468
School: (718) 960-5115
Admissions: (718) 960-5115
Fax: (718) 960-5120

Number of Students: 400

Languages: Beginning and Advanced Spanish, Beginning Italian, with more languages to come.

QUEENS HIGH SCHOOL FOR THE SCIENCES AT YORK COLLEGE

94-20 Guy Brewer Boulevard
Jamaica, New York 11451
School: (718) 657-3181
Admissions: (718) 657-3181
Fax: (718) 657-2579

Number of Students: 400–460

PART I

The Basics

1
Introduction

WHAT IS THE SPECIALIZED HIGH SCHOOLS ADMISSIONS TEST?

The Specialized High Schools Admissions Test—from now on, we'll refer to it simply as the SHSAT—helps determine admissions for Stuyvesant High School; the Bronx High School of Science; Brooklyn Technical High School; High School for Math, Science and Engineering at City College; High School of American Studies at Lehman College; and Queens High School for the Sciences at York College. It is a two-and-a-half-hour, multiple-choice test administered to New York City residents in October and November by the New York City Board of Education.

The test is divided into two sections:

1. Verbal section—45 questions, suggested time: 75 minutes

2. Math section—50 questions, suggested time: 75 minutes

You may allot the time differently, as you see fit, but the total may not exceed two and a half hours.

The Verbal section since 1996 has consisted of three types of questions:

1. scrambled paragraphs

2. logical reasoning

3. reading comprehension

The Math section since 1996 has consisted of one type of question (covering several topics):

1. regular multiple-choice math (arithmetic, algebra, and geometry problems)

The answer choices to the questions alternate between ABCDE and FGHJK. Both math and verbal question types will be dealt with in detail in this book. Even though there are two different types of sections on the SHSAT, you will receive one score on the test.

RAW SCORES AND SCALED SCORES

You may hear about two kinds of scores in connection with the SHSAT: raw scores and scaled scores. Here's what they are:

Raw Scores
Your raw score is simply the number of questions you marked correctly. There is no penalty for guessing. If you're not sure of an answer, mark your best guess. The number of questions you answer correctly is used to calculate your final, *scaled* score.

Scaled Scores
The scaled score is your final score. The Board of Education takes your raw score and, in conjunction with a curve, determines your final score on a scale of 200–800. The curve changes annually, so your raw score would result in a different scaled score from year to year. We'll tell you more about scaled scores and what score each school requires in Chapter 2.

How Important Are SHSAT Scores?

The SHSAT is a major determining factor when you apply to one of the Specialized High Schools, but it is not the only one. For those who qualify, there is a Summer Discovery Program that enables students to enter the schools even though their test results were short of the admissions score. To be eligible for this program, a student must (as stated in the *Specialized High Schools Student Handbook*):

1. have scored close to the school's admission score on the SHSAT; and
2. be recommended by his/her counselor, based on any one of the following criteria.
   The student must:
   a. attend a Chapter 1 school and be from a family whose total income is documented as meeting federal income eligibility guidelines established for school food services by the New York State Department of Agriculture, effective July 1, of the year applying; or
   b. be receiving assistance from the Department of Social Services (Welfare); or
   c. be a member of a family whose income is documented as being equivalent to or below Department of Social Services standards; or
   d. be a foster child or ward of the State; or
   e. initially have entered the United States within the last four years and live in a home in which the language customarily spoken is not English.

Students who are successful in meeting the demands of the summer program will be admitted to the school at which they were conditionally accepted.

A Note About Score Improvements

Through our courses, we've found that students' scores usually don't improve gradually. Instead, they tend to go up in spurts, jumping from plateau to plateau. If you work steadily through this book, you too will find yourself improving incrementally. But you'll have to work, and on your own; you won't have a teacher standing over you reminding you to review what you've learned.

Some Warnings

Many of our techniques for beating the SHSAT may seem a bit unorthodox, which means that using them will sometimes require a leap of faith. In order to get the full benefit from our techniques, however, you must trust them, and the best way to develop this trust is to practice the techniques and show yourself that they work.

But you have to practice them properly. If you try our techniques on the practice questions in most popular SHSAT-coaching books, you will probably decide that they don't work. Why?

The practice questions in those books aren't really like the questions on the actual SHSAT. There may be "scrambled paragraphs" and "logical reasoning" in those books, but if you compare them with the questions on real SHSATs, you will discover that they are different. In fact, studying the practice questions and techniques in some of those other books could actually hurt your SHSAT score. In contrast, the practice questions on the diagnostic test in the back of this book are created with the same writing and testing processes that the real test writers use.

We strongly recommend that you get a copy of the *Specialized High Schools Student Handbook*, which is published and given out for free by the folks who write and administer the SHSAT (The New York City Board of Education). The *Specialized High Schools Student Handbook* contains two practice tests. This booklet will give you the opportunity to work on real SHSAT questions, written by the same people at the Board of Education who will write your SHSAT. By practicing our techniques on real SHSATs, you will be able to prove to yourself that they really do work. This will increase your confidence when taking the test.

Another reason to obtain this booklet is that each year the Board of Education reviews the test and decides whether or not to make adjustments to it. This occurs annually in the summer—probably even as you're holding this book in your hands. This means that, while the information we're giving you now was true of the *last* administration of the test, we can't absolutely guarantee that the test will be exactly the same when you take it this year.

But this booklet will tell you what's changed (if anything), and if you use it in conjunction with this book, you'll have covered all the bases.

If you can't get the *Specialized High Schools Student Handbook* at your school, check with your guidance counselor, or call the Board of Education Office of High School Admissions (917-256-4300, 4301) or the Office of Student Support (212-374-2363) for your free copy.

Are you ready? Let's get cracking!

WHAT IS THE PRINCETON REVIEW?

The Princeton Review is the nation's fastest-growing test-preparation company, conducting courses in roughly five hundred locations around the country.

What makes us unique is our techniques, which were developed after analyzing tons of actual standardized tests. We then took these techniques and fine-tuned them by working with hundreds of real students, studying for all types of standardized tests. We don't waste your time with a lot of review that won't improve your score. What we do is show you how to approach the test; in part by teaching you to:

- think like the test writers
- take full advantage of the time allowed
- answer questions correctly by guessing intelligently
- avoid the traps that test writers have laid for you (and use those traps to your advantage!).

You need to do only two things: Trust our techniques and PRACTICE!

2

Everything You Always Wanted to Know About the SHSAT

THE FIRST STEP

Before you begin to think about preparing for the SHSAT, you must complete the essential first step: *Sign up for the test*. It's administered every October. You should register as soon as possible.

Prior to the test (by early September) you must submit an application to the specialized high schools through your school's guidance counselor. You are advised to indicate a first through sixth choice when you take the exam. If you achieve the required score for your first-choice school, that is the specialized high school you're expected to attend; the same goes for your second through sixth choices. Eighth grade students applying for ninth grade admissions will take the test at the end of October. Ninth grade students applying for tenth grade admissions will take the test in early November, and a December/January make-up exam is available to students who can adequately explain why they were unable to take the test in October. For students who move to New York City after the December/January test, a September administration is available. The exact date for this exam can be obtained from either the Board of Education Office of High School Admissions (917-256-4300) or Office of Student Support (212-374-2363).

The test is administered at Stuyvesant, Bronx Science, and Brooklyn Technical, as well as Long Island City High School in Queens. Students take the exam in the borough in which they attend school, except for students in Brooklyn School Districts 13, 14, and 15, and Staten Island District 31, who take the exam at Stuyvesant High School.

EIGHTH VS. NINTH

Primarily, eighth grade students take the test for admission into the ninth grade. There is also, however, a smaller administration of the test for ninth graders (for tenth grade admissions) the week after the eighth grade test.

The difference between the eighth and ninth grade tests is in the difficulty of the math questions and the complexity of the verbal questions. There are also some small differences in content. For instance, sentence structure on the eighth grade test is less challenging than on the ninth grade test. In math, you will see similar general concepts tested (arithmetic, algebra, geometry, charts, and graphs), but the ninth grade test will also test additional topics such as slope, three dimensional geometry, factorials, and basic trigonometry.

ABOUT YOUR SCORE

What follows is some complex information that will be helpful in interpreting your SHSAT scores, as well as increasing them. We'll provide data about scoring and the scaled score needed for admittance for each of the specialized high schools. If you have a particular SHSAT score goal in mind now, that's great. This information will help you figure out exactly what you need to do in order to reach your goal.

If you have taken a practice test already, you can use your score on that test to determine your starting point. If you haven't had the chance to take a practice test, that's no problem. You can take the lowest target score and make it your goal, at least until you have had a chance to take a practice test and see how you're doing.

Raw score vs. scaled score

Your raw score is the number of math questions you answered correctly added to the number of verbal questions you answered correctly. Since there are 50 math questions and 45 verbal questions with a total of 50 points, your highest possible raw score is 100. This total is then converted to a scaled score between 200 and 800. From 1994 through 2001, the scaled minimum scores remained fairly steady at 559–560 for admittance to Stuyvesant, 508–510 for Bronx Science, and 470–471 for Brooklyn Tech.

In the fall of 2002, with the introduction of the High School for Math, Science and Engineering at City College, the High School of American Studies at Lehman College, and the Queens High School for the Sciences at York College, the acceptance structure changed.

The following is an approximation of how the students were placed. The top scorers who chose Stuyvesant as their first choice were admitted until the incoming class was filled (approximately 750 students). Those students who may have scored high enough for admittance to Stuyvesant, but placed one of the other schools as their first preference, were admitted to that school of choice. So make sure you and your parents are clear about what your preferences are. We estimate the low end of the Stuyvesant class scored around 571 in 2002. The Bronx Science class was filled with approximately 650 students. We estimate the low end of the Bronx Science class scored around 533 that year. For the approximatley 1490 other students their scores were above the minimum cut off of 506 for Brooklyn Tech, City College, Lehman, and York. As you can see, predicting a scaled score from a raw score is problematic.

Now the question on the tip of your tongue is probably something along the lines of, "Hey Princeton Review, so how many questions DO I need to answer correctly to get accepted?" Unfortunately there's a lack of concrete information we can give you. The Board of Education doesn't release their conversion tables from year to year. So anyone who doesn't work for the Board of Education and tells you an exact conversion is, at best, bending the truth. Here is the best guidance we can give you for a target score based on the results of our students over the years:

To achieve the cut off for Stuyvesant: Have a target of 89–92 or more to be in range.

To achieve the cut off for Bronx Science: Have a target of 78–82 or more to be in range.

To achieve the cut off for Brooklyn Tech,
City College, Lehman, and York: Have a target of 64–68 or more to be in range.

These target scores are not guarantees for acceptance. As previously stated, the numbers depend on who is taking the test in a particular year and how well the top scorers perform.

If you have any questions about what this means, don't hesitate to ask your parents, your teacher, or anyone else to help you. Believe it or not, figuring out what your SHSAT scores mean can sometimes be more difficult than most of the math questions on the test!

PART ◆ II

Subject Review

3

SHSAT Pacing

PACING

Most people believe that in order to do well on a test, it is important to answer every question. While this is true of most of the tests you take in school, it is not true of many standardized tests, including the SHSAT. On this test, it is possible to score well without answering all of the questions. In fact, many students can improve their scores by answering fewer questions.

Wait a second, you're thinking, *I can get a better score by doing less of the test?* Yes. The reason for this is that, in an effort to answer all the questions, many students rush through the easy questions, making careless errors. They then spend more of their time on harder questions, which they are likely to answer incorrectly anyway. The trick is to answer fewer questions, but get more of the questions that you do answer right. If you don't finish every question on the test, that's fine, because by working slowly and carefully you will score higher than you would have by rushing to answer more questions. However, since there's *no* guessing penalty, choose an answer for all of the questions.

PROCESS OF ELIMINATION

What is the capital of Malawi?

- (A) New York
- (B) Paris
- (C) London
- (D) Lilongwe
- (E) Washington, DC

There are two ways to get this question right. First, you can just know that the capital of Malawi is Lilongwe. If you do, good for you! The second is to know that the capital of Malawi is not New York, Paris, London, or Washington, DC. Here, you don't get more points for knowing the right answer from the start, so one way is just as good as the other. Try to get in the habit of looking at a question and asking, "What are the wrong answers?" instead of "What is the right answer?"

By using the Process of Elimination (or POE), you can eliminate wrong answers and then have fewer answers from which to pick. The result is that you will pick right answers more often.

GUESSING

The SHSAT has no guessing penalty, meaning that there's no wrong answer penalty. If a student guessed randomly, he/she would guess the correct answer one time out of five. So if you can't eliminate any answers for a question, you should just go ahead and pick one.

If you encounter a verbal question to which you do not know the right answer, don't just give up and leave it blank. Instead, look at the answer choices and try to identify wrong answers so you can eliminate them. Using POE turns guessing into a way to improve your score. If you can eliminate even one out of five answer choices, the odds are then in your favor to take a guess.

A QUICK SUMMARY

These techniques are important enough that we want to mention them again. Make sure you understand these points about the SHSAT before you go any farther in the book.

- Taking your time to answer questions slowly and carefully can improve your test score. Don't rush through the easy answers.

- You will not immediately know the correct answer to every question. Instead, use POE and look for wrong answers that you can eliminate.

- There is no penalty for guessing on the SHSAT. So don't leave anything blank—always choose something!

Educated guessing is a good thing and it will improve your score. As a general rule of thumb, if you invest enough time to read and think about the answer to a question, you should be able to eliminate at least one choice and take a *good* guess!

HOW TO USE THE TARGET SCORES (FROM CHAPTER 2)

As we mentioned, slowing down and skipping questions will increase your score. By using the target scores, you can see how much of the test you have to answer to gain admission to the school you desire. For Brooklyn Tech, Bronx Science, City College, Lehman or York, it's counterproductive to finish the whole test; you will be much better off skipping questions along the way. This will give you the opportunity to correctly answer all the questions that are easiest to you. For Stuyvesant you can afford to skip only a few questions, so omit the few that really give you trouble, but remember that for any question that you skip you should still take a guess and write something in.

4

SHSAT Math

INTRODUCTION

This section will provide you with a review of all the math that you need to take the SHSAT. When you get started, you may feel that the material is too easy. Don't worry. The SHSAT measures your basic math skills, so although you might feel a little frustrated reviewing something you've already learned, this is undoubtedly the best way to improve your score.

We recommend that you work straight through this math review chapter, first reviewing each concept and then doing each set of drills. If you have trouble with one section, mark the page so you can return to it later and go over it again. Keep in mind that you shouldn't breeze over pages or sections just because they look familiar. Take the time to read over the entire chapter so you'll be sure to know all the math you'll need!

Lose Your Calculator

You will not be allowed to use a calculator on the SHSAT. If you have developed a habit of reaching for your calculator whenever you need to add or multiply a couple of numbers, follow our advice: Put your calculator away now and take it out again after the test is behind you. Trust us, you'll be glad you did.

Write It Down

Do not try to do math in your head. You are allowed to write in your test booklet. You *should* write in your test booklet. Even when you are just adding a few numbers together, write them down and do the work on paper. Not only will writing things down help eliminate careless errors, it will also give you something to refer to if you need to check over your work.

One Pass, Two Pass

Within any Math section, you will find three types of questions:

- those you can answer easily without spending very much time

- those which, if you had all the time in the world, you could do

- those that you have absolutely no idea how to tackle

When you work on a Math section, start out with the first question. If you think you can do it without too much trouble, go ahead. If not, save it for later. Move on to the second question and decide whether to do that one. In general, the questions in each Math section are in a very rough order of difficulty. This means that earlier questions tend to be somewhat easier than later ones. You will likely find yourself answering more questions toward the beginning of the section and guessing more toward the end.

Once you've made it all the way through the section, working slowly and carefully doing all the questions that come easily for you, go back and try some of the ones that you think you can do, but will take a little longer. Hopefully you will pace yourself so that while you're working on the second pass through the section, time will run out. You won't be frustrated, though, because you'll know that you answered all the questions that were easy for you. Using a two-pass system and knowing that you can do the questions in whatever order you like is good, smart test taking.

GUESSTIMATING

Sometimes accuracy is important. Sometimes it isn't.

Which of the following fractions is less than $\frac{1}{4}$?

(A) $\frac{4}{18}$

(B) $\frac{4}{12}$

(C) $\frac{7}{7}$

(D) $\frac{10}{9}$

(E) $\frac{12}{5}$

Without doing a bit of calculation, think about this question. It asks you to find a fraction smaller than $\frac{1}{4}$. Even if you're not sure which one is actually smaller, you can certainly use POE to eliminate some wrong answers.

Start simple: $\frac{1}{4}$ is less than 1, right? Are there any fractions in the answer choices that are greater than 1? Get rid of (D) and (E).

Look at answer choice (C). $\frac{7}{7}$ equals 1. Can it be less than $\frac{1}{4}$? Eliminate (C). Already, without doing any math, you have a 50 percent chance of guessing the right answer.

Here's another good example:

A group of three men buys a one-dollar lottery ticket that wins $400. If the one dollar they paid for the ticket is subtracted and the remainder of the prize money is divided equally among the men, how much will each man receive?

(A) $62.50
(B) $75.00
(C) $100.00
(D) $133.00
(E) $200.00

This isn't a terribly difficult question. To solve it mathematically, you would take $400, subtract $1, and then divide the remainder by three. But by using a little bit of logic, you don't have to do any of that.

The lottery ticket won $400. If there were four men, each one would have won about $100 (actually slightly less because the problem tells you to subtract the $1 price of the ticket, but you get the idea). So far so good?

There weren't four men, though; there were only three. This means fewer men among whom to divide the winnings, so each one should get more than $100, right? Look at the answer choices. Eliminate (A), (B), and (C).

Two choices left. Answer choice (E) is $200.00, half of the amount of the winning ticket? If there were three men, could each one get half? Unfortunately not. Eliminate (E). What's left? The right answer!

Guesstimating also works very well with some geometry questions, but just to give you something you can look forward to, we'll save that for the Geometry chapter.

FUNDAMENTALS

MATH VOCABULARY

Many of the math questions on the SHSAT are word problems. If you're going to do well, you need to make sure you know what the words mean. This table lists some of the most popular math vocabulary words used on these tests. Make sure you know all of them!

Term	Definition	Examples
Integer	Any number that does not contain either a fraction or a decimal.	14, 3, 0, –3
Positive Number	Any number greater than zero.	½, 1, 104
Negative Number	Any number less than zero.	–½, –1, –104
Even Number	Any number that is evenly divisible by two. Zero is an even number!	104, 16, 2, 0, –104
Odd Number	Any number that is not evenly divisible by two.	115, 11, 1, –1, –11, –115
Prime Number	Any number that is only divisible by 1 and itself. **NOTE:** One is not a prime number.	2, 3, 5, 7, 13, 131
Digit	The numbers from 0 through 9.	0, 2, 3, 7
Consecutive Number	Any series of numbers listed in the order in which they appear on the number line.	3, 4, 5, or –1, 0, 1, 2
Distinct Numbers	Numbers that are different from one another.	2, 7, 19 are three distinct numbers. 4 and 4 are not distinct because they are the same number
Sum	The result of addition.	The sum of 6 and 2 is 8 because $6 + 2 = 8$.
Difference	The result of subtraction.	The difference between 6 and 2 is 4 because $6 - 2 = 4$.
Product	The result of multiplication.	The product of 6 and 2 is 12 because $6 \times 2 = 12$.
Quotient	The result of division	The quotient when 6 is divided by 2 is 3, because $6 \div 2 = 3$.
Square	The result of multiply a number by itself.	$6^2 = 6 \times 6 = 36$

Practice — Math vocabulary test (the answers are on p. 106)

1. How many integers are there between –1 and 6?_____

2. List three consecutive even integers:_____

3. How many odd integers are there between 1 and 9? _____

4. What is the tens digit in the number 182.09?_____

5. The product of any number and the smallest positive integer is:

   _____

6. What is the product of 5, 6, and 3?_____

7. What is the sum of 3, 11, and 16?_____

8. What is the difference between your answer to number 6 and your answer to number 7?_____

9. List three consecutive positive even numbers:_____

10. Is 11 a prime number?_____

11. What is the sum of the digits in the number 5,647? _____

12. The sum of five consecutive positive integers is 30. What is the square of the largest of the five positive integers?

    (A) 25
    (B) 36
    (C) 49
    (D) 64
    (E) 81

ORDER OF OPERATIONS

How would you attack this problem?

$$16 - 45 \ (2 + 1)^2 \times 4 + 5 =$$

To solve a problem like this, use PEMDAS. The order of operations is:

	Parentheses
	Exponents
Done at the same time from left to right {	Multiplication
	Division
	Addition
	Subtraction } Done at the same time from left to right

You can remember the order of operations using this phrase:

Please Excuse My Dear Aunt Sally.

Now, let's give it a try:
$$16 - 45 \div (2 + 1)^2 \times 4 + 5 =$$

1. PARENTHESES:

$$16 - 45 \div \underline{(2 + 1)}^2 \times 4 + 5 =$$

$$16 - 45 \div (\mathbf{3})^2 \times 4 + 5 =$$

2. EXPONENTS:

$$16 - 45 \div (3)^2 \times 4 + 5 =$$

$$16 - 45 \div \mathbf{9} \times 4 + 5 =$$

3. MULTIPLICATION AND DIVISION (from left to right):

$$16 - \underline{45 \div 9} \times 4 + 5 =$$

$$16 - \underline{5 \times 4} + 5 =$$

$$16 - \mathbf{20} + 5 =$$

4. ADDITION AND SUBTRACTION (from left to right):

$$\underline{16 - 20} + 5 =$$

$$\mathbf{-4} + 5 = \boxed{1}$$

Just take it one step at a time and the math is easy!

Practice — Order of operations (the answers are on p. 106)

1. $10 - 3 + 2 =$

2. $15 + (7 - 3) - 3 =$

3. $3 \times 2 + 3 \div 3 =$

4. $2 \times (4 + 6) \div 4 =$

5. $420 \div (5 \times 12 + 10) =$

6. $20 \times 5 \div 10 + 20 =$

7. $(3 + 5) \times 10 \times 7 \div 8 =$

8. $10 \times (8 + 1) \times (3 + 1) \div (8 - 2) =$

9. $12 \div 2 \div 2 \times 5 + 5 =$

10. $200 - 150 \div 3 \times 2 =$

FACTORS

Factors are all the numbers that divide evenly into your original number. For example, two is a factor of ten; it goes in five times. Three is not a factor of ten because ten divided by three does not produce an integer quotient (and therefore does not "go in evenly"). When asked to find the factors of a number, just make a list.

The factors of 16 are:
    1 and 16   (always start with 1 and the original number)
    2 and 8
    4 and 4
    Is 3 a factor of 16? <u>NO</u>

The factors of 18 are:
    1 and 18
    2 and 9
    3 and 6

Knowing some rules of divisibility can save you some time.

A Number Is Divisible By	If...
2	If it ends in 0, 2, 4, 6, or, 8.
3	If the sum of the digits is divisible by 3.
5	If it ends in 0 or 5.
9	If the sum of the digits is divisible by 9.
10	If it ends in 0.

Practice — Factors (the answers are on p. 106)

1. How many factors does the number 24 have?

    (A) 2
    (B) 4
    (C) 6
    (D) 8
    (E) 10

2. If 12 is a factor of a certain number, which must also be factors of that number?

(F) 2 and 6 only
(G) 3 and 4 only
(H) 12 only
(J) 1, 2, 3, 4, and 6
(K) 1, 2, 3, 4, 6, and 24

3. What is the smallest number that can be added to the number 1,024 to produce a result divisible by 9?

(A) 1
(B) 2
(C) 3
(D) 4
(E) 6

MULTIPLES

Multiples result when you multiply your number by any integer. Fifteen is a multiple of five because five times three equals fifteen. Eighteen is a multiple of three, but not a multiple of five. Another way to think about multiples is to consider them "counting by a number."

The first seven positive multiples of 7 are:

7	(7×1)
14	(7×2)
21	(7×3)
28	(7×4)
35	(7×5)
42	(7×6)
49	(7×7)

Practice — Multiples (the answers are on p. 106)

1. Which of the following is a multiple of 3?

(A) 2
(B) 6
(C) 10
(D) 14
(E) 16

2. Which of the following is NOT a multiple of 6?

(F) 12
(G) 18
(H) 24
(J) 23
(K) 42

3. Which of the following is a multiple of both 3 and 5?

    (A) 10
    (B) 20
    (C) 25
    (D) 45
    (E) 50

4. A company's profit was $75,000 in 1972. In 1992, its profit was $450,000. The profit in 1992 was how many times as great as the profit in 1972?

    (F) 2
    (G) 4
    (H) 6
    (J) 10
    (K) 60

FRACTIONS

A fraction really just tells you to divide. For instance, $\frac{5}{8}$ actually means five divided by eight (which equals 0.625 as a decimal).

Another way to think of this is to imagine a pie cut into eight pieces, $\frac{5}{8}$ tells you something about five of those eight pieces of pie.

The parts of a fraction are called the numerator and the denominator. The numerator is the number on top of the fraction; it refers to the *part* of the pie. The denominator is on the bottom of the fraction and tells you how many pieces there are in the entire pie.

$$\frac{numerator}{denominator}$$

Reducing fractions

Imagine a pie cut into two big pieces. You eat one of the pieces. That means that you have eaten $\frac{1}{2}$ of the pie. Now imagine the same pie cut into four pieces; you eat two. That's $\frac{2}{4}$ this time. But look: The two fractions are equivalent!

To reduce fractions, just divide the top number and the bottom number by the same number. Start out with small numbers like 2, 3, 5, or 10 and reduce again if you need to.

$$\frac{12}{24} \div \frac{2}{2} = \frac{6}{12} \div \frac{2}{2} = \frac{3}{6} \div \frac{3}{3} = \frac{1}{2}$$

In this example if you happened to see that both 12 and 24 were divisible by 12, then you could have saved two quick steps. Don't spend very much time, though, looking for the biggest number possible by which to reduce a fraction. If you start out with a small number, doing one extra set of reducing doesn't take very much time and will definitely help prevent careless errors.

Practice — Reducing fractions (the answers are on p.107)

1. $\dfrac{6}{8} =$

2. $\dfrac{12}{60} =$

3. $\dfrac{20}{30} =$

4. $\dfrac{36}{96} =$

5. $\dfrac{24}{32} =$

6. $\dfrac{16}{56} =$

7. $\dfrac{1056}{1056} =$

8. $\dfrac{154}{126} =$

9. What does it mean when the numerator is bigger than the denominator?

Adding and subtracting fractions with a common denominator

To add or subtract fractions with a common denominator, just add or subtract the top numbers and leave the bottom number alone.

$$\frac{5}{7} + \frac{1}{7} = \frac{6}{7}$$

$$\frac{5}{7} - \frac{1}{7} = \frac{4}{7}$$

Adding and subtracting fractions when the denominators are different

In the past, you have probably tried to randomly search for common denominators so that you could just add or subtract straight across. There is an easier way; it is called the *Bowtie*.

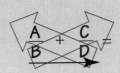

This diagram may make the Bowtie look complicated. It's not. There are three simple steps to adding and subtracting fractions with different denominators.

Step 1: Multiply diagonally going up.
First **B** × **C**. Write the product next to **C**.
Then **D** × **A**. Write the product next to **A**.

Step 2: Multiply straight across the bottom, **B** × **D**.
Write their product as the denominator in your answer.

Step 3: For addition, add the numbers written next to **A** and **C**.
Write the sum as the numerator in your answer.

For subtraction, subtract the numbers written next to **A** and **C**. Write the difference as the numerator in your answer.

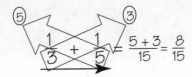

Practice—Adding and subtracting fractions (the answers are on p. 107)

1. $\dfrac{3}{8} + \dfrac{2}{3} =$

2. $\dfrac{1}{3} + \dfrac{3}{8} =$

3. $\dfrac{4}{7} + \dfrac{2}{7} =$

4. $\dfrac{3}{4} - \dfrac{2}{3} =$

5. $\dfrac{7}{9} + \dfrac{5}{4} =$

6. $\dfrac{2}{5} - \dfrac{3}{4} =$

7. $\dfrac{10}{12} + \dfrac{7}{2} =$

8. $\dfrac{17}{27} - \dfrac{11}{27} =$

9. $\dfrac{3}{20} + \dfrac{2}{3} =$

10. $\dfrac{x}{3} + \dfrac{4x}{6} =$

Multiplying fractions

Multiplying is the easiest thing to do with fractions. All you need to do is multiply straight across the top and bottom.

$$\frac{3}{7} \times \frac{4}{5} = \frac{3 \times 4}{7 \times 5} = \frac{12}{35}$$

Dividing fractions

Dividing fractions is almost as simple as multiplying. You just have to flip the second fraction and then multiply.

$$\frac{3}{8} \div \frac{2}{5} = \frac{3}{8} \times \frac{5}{2} = \frac{15}{16}$$

When dividing, don't ask why; just flip the second fraction and multiply!

Practice—Multiplying and dividing fractions (the answers are on p. 108)

1. $\dfrac{2}{3} \times \dfrac{1}{2} =$

2. $\dfrac{5}{8} \div \dfrac{1}{2} =$

3. $\dfrac{4}{5} \times \dfrac{3}{10} =$

4. $\dfrac{24}{15} \times \dfrac{10}{16} =$

5. $\dfrac{16}{25} \div \dfrac{4}{5} =$

Practice — Fraction problems (the answers are on p. 108)

1. Joanna owns one-third of the pieces of furniture in the apartment she shares with her friends. If there is a total of twelve pieces of furniture in the apartment, how many pieces does Joanna own?

    (A) 2
    (B) 4
    (C) 6
    (D) 8
    (E) 12

2. A tank of oil is one-third full. When full, the tank holds 90 gallons. How many gallons of oil are in the tank now?

    (F) 10
    (G) 20
    (H) 30
    (J) 40
    (K) 50

3. Tigger the Cat sleeps three-fourths of every day. In a four-day period, he sleeps the equivalent of how many full days?

    (A) $\dfrac{1}{4}$

    (B) $\dfrac{3}{4}$

    (C) 1

    (D) 3

    (E) 4

4. Which of the following is the greatest?

    (F) $\dfrac{1}{4} + \dfrac{2}{3}$

    (G) $\dfrac{3}{4} - \dfrac{1}{3}$

    (H) $\dfrac{1}{12} \div \dfrac{1}{3}$

    (J) $\dfrac{3}{4} \times \dfrac{1}{3}$

    (K) $\dfrac{1}{12} \times 2$

5. $\dfrac{1}{2} + \dfrac{2}{3} + \dfrac{3}{4} + \dfrac{1}{2} + \dfrac{1}{3} + \dfrac{1}{4} =$

(A) $\dfrac{3}{4}$

(B) 1

(C) 6

(D) 3

(E) 12

DECIMALS

Remember, decimals and fractions are just two different ways of writing the same thing. To change a fraction into a decimal, you just divide the bottom number into the top number.

Be sure you know the names of all the decimal places. Here's a quick reminder:

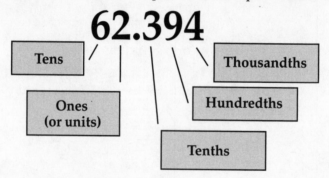

Adding decimals

To add decimals, just line up the decimal places and add.

$$\begin{array}{r} 48.02 \\ +\ \underline{19.12} \\ 67.14 \end{array}$$

Subtracting decimals

To subtract, do the same thing. Line up the decimal places and subtract.

$$\begin{array}{r} 67.14 \\ -\ \underline{48.02} \\ 19.12 \end{array}$$

Multiplying decimals

To multiply decimals, first count the number of digits to the right of the decimal point in the numbers you are multiplying. Then just multiply and move the decimal point in your answer from right to left by the same number of spaces.

$$
\begin{array}{r}
0.5 \\
\times\ 4.2 \\
\hline
1\ 0 \\
2\ 0 \\
\hline
2.10
\end{array}
$$

(two digits to the right of the decimal point)

Dividing decimals

To divide, move the decimal points in both numbers the same number of spaces to the right until you are working only with integers. Look at this problem:

$$12.5 \div 0.25 = 0.25\overline{)12.5}$$

Move both decimals over two places and start dividing.

$$25\overline{)1250} \quad \frac{50}{}$$

Practice — Decimals (the answers are on p. 108)

1. $1.43 + 17.27 =$

2. $2.49 + 1.7 =$

3. $7.08 - 2.3 =$

4. $4.25 \times 2.5 =$

5. $.02 \times .90 =$

6. $180 \div .03 =$

7. $.10 \div .02 =$

8. The product of .34 and 1000 is approximately
   - (A) 3.50
   - (B) 35
   - (C) 65
   - (D) 350
   - (E) 650

9. $2.398 =$

(F) $2 \times \dfrac{9}{100} \times \dfrac{3}{10} \times \dfrac{8}{1000}$

(G) $2 + \dfrac{3}{10} + \dfrac{9}{1000} + \dfrac{8}{100}$

(H) $2 + \dfrac{9}{10} + \dfrac{8}{1000} + \dfrac{3}{10}$

(J) $\dfrac{3}{10} + \dfrac{9}{100} + \dfrac{8}{1000}$

(K) None of the above

EXPONENTS

Exponents are just another way to indicate multiplication. For instance, 3^2 simply means to multiply three by itself, so $3^2 = 3 \times 3 = 9$. Even higher exponents aren't very complicated.

For example: $2^5 = 2 \times 2 \times 2 \times 2 \times 2 = 32$.

The questions on the SHSAT don't generally use exponents higher than four or five, so this is likely to be as complicated as it gets.

The rule for exponents is simple: When in doubt, write it out! Don't try to figure out two times two times two times two times two in your head (just look at how silly it looks written in words!). Instead, write it as a math problem and just work through it one step at a time.

What would you do if you were asked to solve this problem?

$$Q^3 \times Q^2 =$$

Let's look at this one carefully. Q^3 means $Q \times Q \times Q$ and Q^2 means $Q \times Q$. Put them together and you've got:

$$(Q \times Q \times Q) \times (Q \times Q) =$$

How many Qs is that? Count them. Five! Be careful, when multiplying exponents like this, that you don't get confused and multiply the actual exponents, which would give you Q^6. If you are ever unsure, don't spend a second worrying; just write out the expression for the exponent and count the number of things you are multiplying.

Practice — Exponents (the answers are on p. 108)

1. $2^3 =$

2. $2^4 =$

3. $3^3 =$

4. $4^3 =$

5. $2^3 \times 2^3 \times 2^2 =$

    (A) 64
    (B) 2^8
    (C) 2^{10}
    (D) 2^{16}
    (E) 2^{18}

6. For what integer value of m does $2m + 4 = m^3$?

    (F) 1
    (G) 2
    (H) 3
    (J) 4
    (K) 5

ALGEBRA

MANIPULATING AN EQUATION

In order to solve an equation, you must first isolate the variable, meaning that you want to get the variable on one side of the equation and everything else on the other side.

$$3x + 5 = 17$$

To do this, follow these two steps:

Step 1: Move elements around using addition and subtraction.
Get variables on one side and numbers on the other.
Simplify.

Step 2: Divide both sides of the equation by the *coefficient*, the number in front of the variable. If that number is a fraction, multiply everything by the denominator.

For example:

$$\begin{aligned}3x + 5 &= 17 \\ -5 &\quad -5 \\ \hline 3x &= 12 \\ \div 3 &= \div 3 \\ \hline x &= 4\end{aligned}$$

Subtract 5 from both sides to get rid of the numbers on the left side.

Divide both sides by 3 to get rid of the 3 on the left side. Done!

Whatever you do to one side, you must also do to the other.

Practice — Manipulate (the answers are on p. 109)

1. If $6 + 2 = 11 - x$, then $x =$

2. If $4x = 20$, then $x =$

3. If $5x - 20 = 10$, then $x =$

4. If $4x + 3 = 31$, then $x =$

5. If $m + 5 = 3m - 3$, then $m =$

6. If $2.5x = 20$, then $x =$

7. If $0.2x + 2 = 3.6$, then $x =$

8. If $6 = 8x + 4$, then $x =$

9. If $3(x + y) = 21$, then $x + y =$

10. If $3x + 3y = 21$, then $x + y =$

11. If $50 + 3(40 - 5y) = 65$, then $y =$

12. One-fifth of the students in a class chose recycling as the topic for their science projects. If four students chose recycling, how many students are in the class?
    (A) 4
    (B) 10
    (C) 16
    (D) 20
    (E) 24

13. If $6x - 4 = 38$, then $x + 10 =$
    (F) 7
    (G) 10
    (H) 16
    (J) 17
    (K) 19

14. If $3x - 6 = 21$, then what is $x \times 9$?
    (A) 0
    (B) 1
    (C) 3
    (D) 6
    (E) 9

15. Only one-fifth of the chairs in a classroom are in working order. If three extra chairs are brought in, there are 19 working seats available. How many chairs were originally in the room?

    (F) 16
    (G) 19
    (H) 22
    (J) 80
    (K) 95

FUNCTIONS

A function is just a set of instructions written in a strange way.

$$\# x = 3x(x + 1)$$

On the left:	there is usually a variable with a strange symbol next to or around it.
In the middle:	is an equal sign.
On the right:	are the instructions. These tell you what to do with the variable.

$\# x = 3x(x + 1)$	*What does # 5 equal?*
$\# 5 = 3 \times 5(5 + 1)$	*Just replace each x with a 5.*

Here the function (indicated by the # sign) simply tells you to substitute a 5 wherever there was an x in the original set of instructions. Functions look confusing because of the strange symbols, but once you know what to do with them, they are just like equations.

Sometimes more than one question will refer to the same function. The following drill, for example, contains two questions about one function. In cases such as this, the first question tends to be easier than the second.

Practice — Functions (the answers are on p. 109)
Questions 1–2 refer to the following definition.

For all real numbers n, $\$n = 10n - 10$

1. $\$7 =$

    (A) 70
    (B) 60
    (C) 17
    (D) 7
    (E) 0

2. If $\$n = 120$, then $n =$

    (F) 11
    (G) 12
    (H) 13
    (J) 120
    (K) 130

Questions 3–5 refer to the following definition.

For all real numbers d and y, $d \text{ ¿ } y = (d \times y) - (d + y)$.

[Example: $3 \text{ ¿ } 2 = (3 \times 2) - (3 + 2) = 6 - 5 = 1$]

3. $10 \text{ ¿ } 2 =$

    (A) 20
    (B) 16
    (C) 12
    (D) 8
    (E) 4

4. If $K (4 \text{ ¿ } 3) = 30$, then $K =$

    (F) 3
    (G) 4
    (H) 5
    (J) 6
    (K) 7

5. $(2 \text{ ¿ } 4) \times (3 \text{ ¿ } 6) =$

    (A) $(9 \text{ ¿ } 3) + 3$
    (B) $(6 \text{ ¿ } 4) + 1$
    (C) $(5 \text{ ¿ } 3) + 4$
    (D) $(8 \text{ ¿ } 4) + 2$
    (E) $(9 \text{ ¿ } 4) + 3$

PERCENTAGES

Solving percent problems is easy when you know how to translate them from "percent language" into "math language." Once you've done the translation, you guessed it—just manipulate the equation!

60% of what is 24?

Percent Language	Math Language
% or "percent"	Out of 100 ($\frac{x}{100}$)
Of	Times (as in Multiplication)($\times$)
What	Your favorite variable (p)
Is, are, were	Equals ($=$)

Whenever you see the percent words from this table, just translate them into math language and go to work on the equation!

For example:

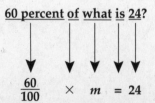

Practice — Translating and solving percent questions (the answers are on p. 109)

1. 30 is what percent of 250?

2. What is 12% of 200?

3. What is 25% of 10% of 200?

4. 75% of 20% of what is 12?

Practice — Word problems involving percentages (the answers are on p. 109)

1. If a harvest yielded 60 bushels of corn, 20 bushels of wheat, and 40 bushels of soybeans, what percent of the total harvest was corn?

   (A) 25%
   (B) 30%
   (C) 33%
   (D) 40%
   (E) 50%

2. At a local store, an item that usually sells for $45 is currently on sale for $30. What discount does that represent?

   (F) 10%
   (G) 25%
   (H) 33%
   (J) 50%
   (K) 66%

3. Which of the following is most nearly 35% of $19.95?

   (A) $13.50
   (B) $9.95
   (C) $7.00
   (D) $5.75
   (E) $3.50

4. Of the fifty hotels in the Hilltop Hotels chain, five have indoor swimming pools and fifteen have outdoor swimming pools. What percent of all Hilltop Hotels have either an indoor or an outdoor swimming pool?

   (F) 5%
   (G) 15%
   (H) 20%
   (J) 30%
   (K) 40%

5. For which price does 40% off equal a $20 discount?

   (A) $50.00
   (B) $100.00
   (C) $400.00
   (D) $800.00
   (E) None of the above.

6. A pair of shoes is offered on a special blowout sale. The original price of the shoes is reduced from $50 to $20. What is the percent change in the price of the shoes?

 (F) 20%
 (G) 25%
 (H) 40%
 (J) 50%
 (K) 60%

7. Lisa buys a silk dress regularly priced at $60, a cotton sweater regularly priced at $40, and four pairs of socks regularly priced at $5 each. If the dress and the socks are on sale for 20% off the regular price and the sweater is on sale for 10% off the regular price, what is the total amount of her purchase?

 (A) $90.00
 (B) $96.00
 (C) $100.00
 (D) $102.00
 (E) $108.00

8. Thirty percent of $17.95 is closest to

 (F) $2.00
 (G) $3.00
 (H) $6.00
 (J) $9.00
 (K) $12.00

9. Fifty percent of the 20 students in Mrs. Schweizer's third grade class are boys. If 90 percent of these boys ride the bus to school, which of the following is the number of boys in Mrs. Schweizer's class who ride the bus to school?

 (A) 9
 (B) 10
 (C) 12
 (D) 16
 (E) 18

10. On a test with 25 questions, Marc scored an 88%. How many questions did Marc answer correctly?

 (F) 22
 (G) 16
 (H) 12
 (J) 4
 (K) 3

RATIOS

A ratio is like a recipe because it tells you how much of different ingredients go into a mixture.

For example:

To make punch, mix two parts grape juice with three parts orange juice.

This ratio tells you that for every two units of grape juice, you will need to add three units of orange juice. It doesn't matter what the units are; if you were working with ounces, you would mix two ounces of grape juice with three ounces of orange juice to get five ounces of punch. If you were working with gallons, you would mix two gallons of grape juice with three gallons of orange juice. How much punch would you have? Five gallons.

To work through a ratio question, first you need to organize the information you are given. Do this using the Ratio Box.

In a club with 35 members, the ratio of boys to girls is 3:2.

Boys	Girls	Total
3	2	5
× 7	× 7	× 7
21	14	35

To complete your Ratio Box, fill in the ratio at the top and the "real world" at the bottom. Then look for a "magic number" that you can multiply by the ratio to get to the real world. That's all there is to it!

Practice — Ratios (the answers are on p. 110)

1. In a jar of lollipops, the ratio of red lollipops to blue lollipops is 3:5. If only red lollipops and blue lollipops are in the jar and if the total number of lollipops in the jar is 56, how many blue lollipops are in the jar?

    (A) 5
    (B) 8
    (C) 21
    (D) 28
    (E) 35

2. At Jed's Country Hotel, there are three types of rooms: singles, doubles, and triples. If the ratio of singles to doubles to triples is 3:4:5, and the total number of rooms is 36, how many doubles are there?

    (F) 4
    (G) 9
    (H) 12
    (J) 24
    (K) 36

3. Matt's Oak Superstore has exactly three times as many large oak desks as small oak desks in its inventory. If the store only sells these two types of desks, which could be the total number of desks in stock?

(A) 10
(B) 13
(C) 16
(D) 18
(E) 25

4. In Janice's tennis club, 8 of the 12 players are right-handed. What is the ratio of right-handed to left-handed players in Janice's club?

(F) 1:2
(G) 2:1
(H) 1:6
(J) 2:3
(K) 3:4

5. One-half of the 400 students at Booth Junior High School are girls. Of the girls at the school, the ratio of those who ride a school bus to those who walk is 7:3. What is the total number of girls who walk to school?

(A) 10
(B) 30
(C) 60
(D) 120
(E) 140

6. A pet goat eats two pounds of goat food and one pound of grass each day. When the goat has eaten a total of fifteen pounds, how many pounds of grass will it have eaten?

(F) 3
(G) 4
(H) 5
(J) 15
(K) 30

AVERAGES

There are three parts of every average problem: total, number, and average. Most SHSATproblems will give you two of the three pieces and ask you to find the third. To help organize the information you are given, use the Average Pie.

The Average Pie organizes all of your information visually. It is easy to see all of the relationships between the pieces of the pie:

- **TOTAL** = (# of items) × (Average)

- **# of items** = $\dfrac{Total}{Average}$

- **Average** = $\dfrac{Total}{\text{\# of items}}$

For example, if your friend went bowling and bowled three games, scoring 71, 90, and 100, here's how you would compute her average score using the Average Pie:

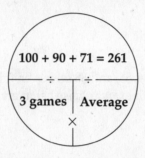

To find the average, you would simply write a fraction that represents , $\dfrac{Total}{\text{\# of items}}$ in this case $\dfrac{261}{3}$.

The math becomes simple. 261 ÷ 3 = 87. Your friend bowled an average of 87.

Get used to working with the Average Pie by using it to solve these problems:

Practice — Average problems (the answers are on p. 110)

1. The average of three numbers is eighteen. What is two times the sum of the three numbers?

    (A) 108
    (B) 54
    (C) 36
    (D) 18
    (E) 6

2. If Set M contains four positive integers whose average is 7, what is the largest number that Set M could contain?

    (F) 6
    (G) 7
    (H) 18
    (J) 25
    (K) 28

3. An art club of 4 boys and 5 girls makes craft projects. If the boys average 2 projects each and the girls average 3 projects each, what is the total number of projects produced by the club?

    (A) 14
    (B) 23
    (C) 26
    (D) 54
    (E) 100

4. If a class of 6 students has an average grade of 72 before a seventh student joins the class, what must the seventh student's grade be in order to raise the class average to 76?

    (F) 76
    (G) 80
    (H) 88
    (J) 92
    (K) 100

5. Catherine scores an 84, 85, and 88 on her first three exams. What must she score on her fourth exam to raise her average to an 89?

    (A) 89
    (B) 91
    (C) 93
    (D) 97
    (E) 99

PLUGGING IN

The SHSAT will often ask you questions about real-life situations where the numbers have been replaced with variables. One of the easiest ways to tackle these questions is by using a powerful technique called Plugging In.

> Mark is two inches taller than John, who is four inches shorter than Evan. If e represents Evan's height in inches, then in terms of j, an expression for Mark's height is:
>
> (A) $e + 6$
> (B) $e + 4$
> (C) $e + 2$
> (D) e
> (E) $e - 2$

The problem with this question is that we're not used to thinking of people's heights in terms of variables. Whenever you see variables used in the question and in the answer choices, just plug in a number to replace the variable.

1. Choose a number for e.

2. Using that number, figure out Mark's and John's heights.

3. Put a box around Mark's height, since that's what the question asked you for.

4. Plug your number for e into the answer choices and choose the one that represents Mark's height.

Here's how it works

Mark is two inches taller than John, who is four inches shorter than Evan. If *e* represents Evan's height in inches, then <u>in terms of *j*</u>, an expression for Mark's height is:

(A) $e + 6$
(B) $e + 4$
(C) $e + 2$
(D) e
(E) $e - 2$

> *Ignore this! Because you are plugging in, you don't need to pay any attention to "in terms of" any variable.*

For Evan's height, let's pick 60 inches. This means that $e = 60$.

Remember, there is no right or wrong number to pick. 50 would work just as well as 100.

But given that Evan is 60 inches tall, now we can figure out that since John is four inches shorter than Evan, John's height must be (60 – 4) or 56 inches.

The other piece of information we learn from the problem is that Mark is two inches taller than John. If John's height is 56 inches, that means Mark must be 58 inches tall.

So here's what we've got:

Evan   60 inches = *e*

John   56 inches

Mark   58 inches

Now, the question asks for Mark's height, which is 58 inches. The last step is to go through the answer choices substituting 60 for *e*, and choose the one that equals 58.

(A)	$e + 6$	$60 + 6 = 66$	ELIMINATE
(B)	$e + 4$	$60 + 4 = 64$	ELIMINATE
(C)	$e + 2$	$60 + 2 = 62$	ELIMINATE
(D)	e	60	ELIMINATE
(E)	$e - 2$	$60 - 2 = 58$	PICK THIS ONE!

This is a very long explanation of all the steps involved when you plug in. Don't be tempted to say, "Plugging In takes too long. I can do the problem just as fast if I write equations for each person's age." Writing equations is a fine way to do algebra in school, but on the SHSAT it is a great way to make mistakes.

Practice — Plugging In (the answers are on p. 110)

1. At a charity fund raiser, 200 people each donated *x* dollars. In terms of *x*, what was the total number of dollars donated?

(A) $\dfrac{x}{200}$

(B) 200

(C) $\dfrac{200}{x}$

(D) $200 + x$

(E) $200x$

2. If 10 magazines cost d dollars, how many magazines can be purchased for 3 dollars?

(F) $\dfrac{3d}{10}$

(G) $30d$

(H) $\dfrac{d}{30}$

(J) $\dfrac{30}{d}$

(K) $\dfrac{10d}{3}$

3. The zoo has four times as many monkeys as lions. There are four more lions than there are zebras at the zoo. If z represents the number of zebras in the zoo, then in terms of z, how many monkeys are there in the zoo?

(A) $4z$
(B) $z + 4$
(C) $z + 8$
(D) $4z + 4$
(E) $4z + 16$

Occasionally you may run into a Plugging-In question that doesn't contain variables. These questions usually ask about a percentage or a fraction of some unknown number or price. This is the one time that you should plug in even when you don't see variables in the answer!

Also, be sure you plug in good numbers. Good doesn't mean right, because there's no such thing as a right or wrong number to plug in. A good number is one that makes the problem easier to work with. If a question asks about minutes and hours, try plugging in 30 or 60, not 128. Also, whenever you see the word "percent,"—you guessed it—plug in 100!

4. The price of a suit is reduced by half, then the resulting price is reduced by 10%. The final price is what percent of the original price?

(F) 5%
(G) 10%
(H) 25%
(J) 40%
(K) 45%

5. On Wednesday, Miguel ate one-fourth of a pumpkin pie. On Thursday, he ate one-half of what was left of the pie. What fraction of the entire pie did Miguel eat on Wednesday and Thursday?

(A) $\dfrac{3}{8}$

(B) $\dfrac{1}{2}$

(C) $\dfrac{5}{8}$

(D) $\dfrac{3}{4}$

(E) $\dfrac{7}{8}$

6. If p pieces of candy cost c cents, 10 pieces of candy will cost

(F) $\dfrac{pc}{10}$ cents

(G) $\dfrac{10c}{p}$ cents

(H) $10pc$ cents

(J) $\dfrac{10p}{c}$ cents

(K) $10 + p + c$ cents

7. If J is an odd integer, which of the following must be true?
(A) $(J \div 3) > 1$
(B) $(J - 2)$ is a positive integer.
(C) $2 \times J$ is an even integer.
(D) $J^2 > J$
(E) $J > 0$

8. If m is an even integer, n is an odd integer, and p is the product of m and n, which of the following is always true?

(F) p is a fraction.
(G) p is an odd integer.
(H) p is divisible by 2.
(J) p is between m and n.
(K) p is greater than zero.

BACKSOLVING

Backsolving is similar to Plugging In. When you have *variables* in the answer choices, you plug in. When you have *numbers* in the answer choices, you will generally backsolve. The only time this may get tricky is when you have a question like the one above that asks for a percent or a fraction of some unknown number.

Backsolving works because on a multiple-choice test, the right answer is always one of the answer choices. So, you can plug in numbers from the answer choices, one of which must be correct. Here's an example:

> Nicole baked a batch of cookies. She gave half to her friend Lisa and six to her mother. If she now has eight cookies left, how many did Nicole bake originally?
>
> (A) 8
> (B) 12
> (C) 20
> (D) 28
> (E) 32

See what we mean? It would be hard to just start making up numbers of cookies and hoping that eventually you guessed correctly. However, the number of cookies that Nicole baked originally must be either 8, 12, 20, 28, or 32 (the five answer choices). So pick one—always start with (C)—and then work backward to determine whether or not you have the right choice.

Let's start with (C): Nicole baked 20 cookies. Now work through the events listed in the question.

She had 20 cookies—from answer choice (C)—and she gave half to Lisa. That leaves Nicole with 10 cookies.

What next? She gives 6 to her mom. Now she's got 4 left.

Keep going. The problem says that Nicole now has 8 cookies left. But if she started with 20—answer choice (C)—she would only have 4 left. So is (C) the right answer? No.

No problem. Choose another answer choice and try again. Be smart, though, about which answer choice you pick. When we used the number in (C), Nicole ended up with fewer cookies than we wanted her to have, didn't she? So the right answer must be a number larger than 20, the number we took from (C).

The good news is that the answer choices in most Backsolving questions go in order, so it is easy to pick the next larger or smaller number—you just pick either (B) or (D), depending on which direction you've decided to go.

Back to Nicole and her cookies. We need a number larger than 20. So let's go to answer choice (D)—28.

Nicole started out with 28 cookies. The first thing she did was give half, or 14, to Lisa. That left Nicole with 14 cookies.

Then she gave 6 cookies to her mother. 14 – 6 = 8. Nicole has 8 cookies left over. Keep going with the question. It says "If Nicole now has eight cookies left . . ." She has eight cookies left and, *voila*—she's supposed to have eight cookies left.

What does this mean? It means you've got the right answer! Pick (D) and move on.

If answer choice (D) had not worked, and you were certain that you needed a number larger than answer choice (D), you still would be finished. Because you started with the middle answer choice, and that didn't work, and then you tried the next larger choice, (D), and that didn't work either, you could pick the only answer bigger than (C) that was left, in this case (E), and be done.

This diagram helps illustrate the way you should move through the answer choices and why you should always start out with answer choice (C).

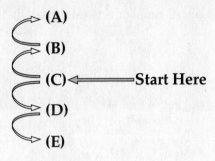

Practice — Backsolving (the answers are on p. 110)

1. Ted can read 60 pages per hour. Naomi can read 45 pages per hour. If both Ted and Naomi read at the same time, how many minutes will it take them to read a total of 210 pages?

   (A) 36
   (B) 72
   (C) 120
   (D) 145
   (E) 180

2. If the sum of y and $y + 1$ is greater than 18, which of the following is one possible value for y?

   (F) –10
   (G) –8
   (H) 2
   (J) 8
   (K) 10

3. Kenny is 5 years older than Greg. In 5 years, Kenny will be twice as old as Greg is now. How old is Kenny now?

   (A) 5
   (B) 10
   (C) 15
   (D) 25
   (E) 35

4. Three people—Paul, Sara, and John—want to put their money together to buy a $90 radio. If Sara agrees to pay twice as much as John, and Paul agrees to pay three times as much as Sara, how much must Sara pay?

   (F) $10
   (G) $20
   (H) $30
   (J) $45
   (K) $65

5. Four less than a certain number is two-thirds of that number. What is the number?

   (A) 1
   (B) 6
   (C) 8
   (D) 12
   (E) 16

GEOMETRY

Guesstimating

Geometry problems are undoubtedly the best places to guesstimate. Unless a particular question tells you that a figure is not drawn to scale, you can safely assume that the figure *is* drawn to scale.

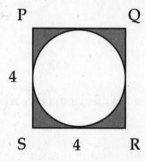

A circle is inscribed in square PQRS. What is the area of the shaded region?

   (A) $16 - 6\pi$
   (B) $16 - 4\pi$
   (C) $16 - 3\pi$
   (D) $16 - 2\pi$
   (E) 16π

Wow, a circle inscribed in a square—that sounds tough!

It isn't. Look at the picture. What fraction of the square looks like it is shaded? Half? Three-quarters? Less than half? In fact, about one-quarter of the area of the square is shaded. You've just done most of the work necessary to solve this problem.

Now, let's do a tiny bit of math. The length of one side of the square is 4, so the area of the square is 4×4 or 16. Don't worry if you feel a little lost; in the next few pages, we'll discuss area in much more detail.

So the area of the square is 16 an d we said that the shaded region was about one-fourth of the square. One-fourth of 16 is 4, right? So we're looking for an answer choice which equals about (not necessarily exactly) 4. Let's look at the choices:

   (A) $16 - 6\pi$
   (B) $16 - 4\pi$
   (C) $16 - 3\pi$
   (D) $16 - 2\pi$
   (E) 16π

This becomes a tiny bit complicated because the answers include π. For the purposes of guesstimating, and in fact for almost any purpose on the SHSAT, you should just remember that π is a little more than 3. Let's look back at those answers:

(A) $16 - 6\pi$	is roughly equal to	$16 - (6 \times 3) = -2$
(B) $16 - 4\pi$	is roughly equal to	$16 - (4 \times 3) = 4$
(C) $16 - 3\pi$	is roughly equal to	$16 - (3 \times 3) = 7$
(D) $16 - 2\pi$	is roughly equal to	$16 - (2 \times 3) = 10$
(E) 16π	is roughly equal to	$(16 \times 3) = 48$

Now let's think about what these answers mean.

Answer choice (A) is geometrically impossible. A figure *cannot* have a negative area. Eliminate it.

Answer choice (B) means that the shaded region has an area of about 4. Sounds pretty good.

Answer choice (C) means that the shaded region has an area of about 7. The area of the entire square was 16, so that would mean that the shaded region was almost half the square. Possible, but doubtful.

Answer choice (D) means that the shaded region has an area of about 10. That's more than half the square and in fact, almost three-quarters of the entire square. No way, cross it out.

Finally, answer choice (E) means that the shaded region has an area of about 48. What? The whole square had an area of 16. Is the shaded region three times as big as the square itself? No shot. Eliminate (E).

At this point you are left with only (B), which we feel pretty good about, and (C), which seems a little big. What should you do?

Pick (B) and pat yourself on the back because you chose the right answer without doing a lot of unnecessary work. Also, remember how useful it was to guesstimate and make sure you do it whenever you see a geometry problem, unless the problem tells you that the figure is not drawn to scale!

PERIMETER

The perimeter is the distance around the outside of any figure. To find the perimeter of a figure, just add up the length of all the sides.

What are the perimeters of these figures?

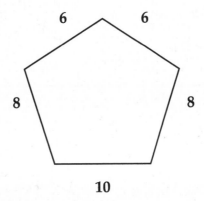

Perimeter = 6 + 6 + 8 + 8 + 10 = 38

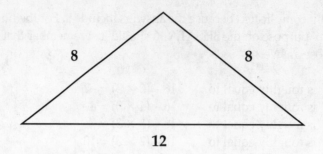

Perimeter = 8 + 8 + 12 = 28

Practice—Perimeter (the answers are on p. 111)

1. A stop sign has 8 equal sides of length 4. What is its perimeter?

    (A) 4
    (B) 8
    (C) 12
    (D) 32
    (E) It cannot be determined from the information given.

2. If the perimeter of a square is 56, what is the length of each side?

    (F) 4
    (G) 7
    (H) 14
    (J) 28
    (K) 112

3. The perimeter of a square with a side of length 4 is how much less than the perimeter of a rectangle with sides of length 4 and width 6?

    (A) 0
    (B) 2
    (C) 4
    (D) 6
    (E) 8

ANGLES

Straight lines

Angles that form a straight line always total 180°.

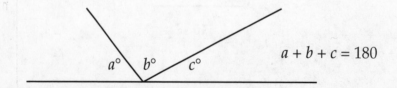

$a + b + c = 180$

Triangles

All the angles in a triangle add up to 180°.

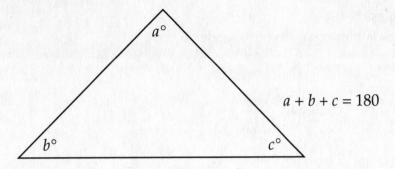

$$a + b + c = 180$$

Four-sided figures

The angles in a square, rectangle, or any other four-sided figure always add up to 360°.

$$p + q + r + s = 360$$

TRIANGLES

Isosceles triangles

Any triangle with two equal sides is an isosceles triangle.

If two sides of a triangle are equal, the angles opposite those sides are always equal.

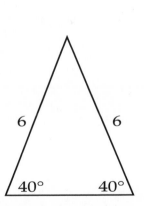

This particular isosceles triangle has two equal sides (of length 6) and therefore two equal angles (40° in this case).

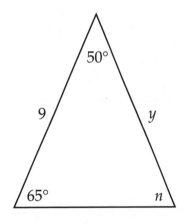

$n = 65°$
$y = 9$

Equilateral triangles

An equilateral triangle is a triangle that has three equal sides. If all the sides are equal, then all the angles must be equal. Each angle in an equilateral triangle equals 60°.

Right triangles

A right triangle is a triangle with one 90° angle.

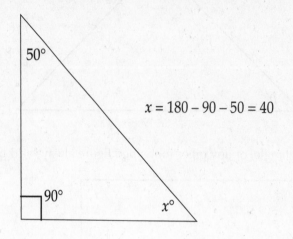

$$x = 180 - 90 - 50 = 40$$

This is a right triangle.
It is also an isosceles triangle.

What does that tell you?

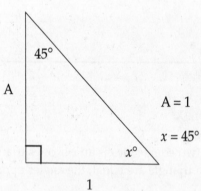

$$A = 1$$

$$x = 45°$$

The Pythagorean theorem

For all right triangles, $a^2 + b^2 = c^2$.

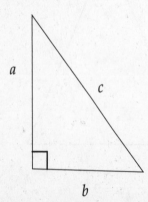

Always remember that c represents the *hypotenuse*, the longest side of the triangle, which is always opposite the right angle.

Test your knowledge of triangles with these problems. If the question describes a figure that isn't shown, make sure you draw the figure yourself!

Practice — Triangles (the answers are on p. 111)

1. What is the perimeter of an equilateral triangle, one side of which measures 4 inches?

   (A) 12 inches
   (B) 8 inches
   (C) 6 inches
   (D) 4 inches
   (E) It cannot be determined from the information given.

2. $x =$

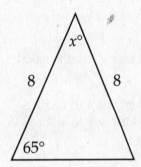

   (F) 8
   (G) 30
   (H) 50
   (J) 65
   (K) 180

3. If $b = 45$, then $v^2 =$

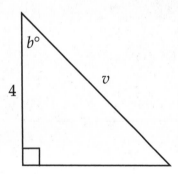

   (A) 32
   (B) 25
   (C) 16
   (D) 5
   (E) It cannot be determined from the information given.

4. One-half of the difference between the number of degrees in a square and the number of degrees in a triangle is

(F) 45
(G) 90
(H) 180
(J) 240
(K) 360

Area

The area is the amount of space taken up by a two-dimensional figure. Area is easy if you think about it in terms of how much space a figure covers on a page. The larger the area, the more paper the figure takes up.

In order to determine the area of a square or rectangle, multiply its length by its width.

area = length × width

What is the area of a rectangle with length 8 and width 6?
In this case, the length is 8 and the width is 6, so 8 × 6 = 48.

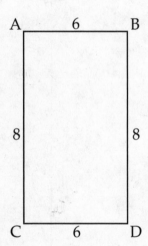

Area of rectangle ABCD = 8 × 6 = 48

To find the area of a triangle, you multiply $\frac{1}{2}$ times the length of the base, times the length of the triangle's height, or $\frac{1}{2}b \times h$.

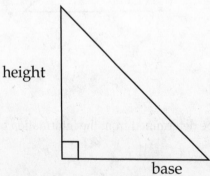

What is the area of a triangle with base 6 and height 3?

(A) 3
(B) 6
(C) 9
(D) 12
(E) 18

Just put the values you are given into the formula and do the math. That's all there is to it!

$$\frac{1}{2}b \times h = \textbf{area}$$

$$(\frac{1}{2})(6) \times 3 = \text{area}$$

$$3 \times 3 = 9$$

The only tricky point you may run into when finding the area of a triangle is when the triangle is not a right triangle. In this case, it becomes slightly more difficult to find the height, which is easiest to think of as the distance to the point of the triangle from the base. Here's an illustration to help:

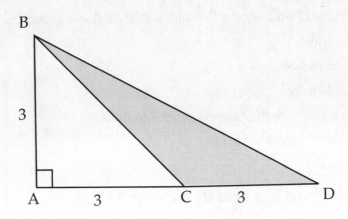

First look at triangle BAC, the unshaded right triangle on the left side. Finding its base and height is simple—they are both 3. So, using our formula for the area of a triangle, we can figure out that the area of triangle BAC is $4\frac{1}{2}$.

Now lets think about triangle BCD, the shaded triangle on the right. It isn't a right triangle, so finding the height will involve a little more thought. Remember the question, though: How far up from the base is the point of triangle BCD? Think of the shaded triangle as sitting on the floor of your room. How far up would its point stick from the ground? Yes, 3! The height of triangle BCD is exactly the same as the height of triangle BAC. Don't worry about drawing lines inside the shaded triangle or anything like that, just figure out how high its point is from the ground.

Okay, to finish up, in order to find the base of triangle BCD (the shaded one) you will use the same area formula, and just plug in 3 for the base and 3 for the height.

$$\frac{1}{2}b \times h = \textbf{area}$$

$$(\frac{1}{2})(3) \times 3 = \text{area}$$

And once you do the math, you'll see that the area of triangle BCD is $4\frac{1}{2}$.

Not quite convinced? Let's look at the question a little differently. The base of the entire figure (triangle DAB) is 6 and the height is 3. Using your trusty area formula, you can figure out that the area of triangle DAB is 9. You know the area of the unshaded triangle is $4\frac{1}{2}$, so what's left for the shaded part? You guessed it: $4\frac{1}{2}$.

VOLUME

Volume is very similar to area, except it takes into account a third dimension. To figure out the volume of a figure, you simply find the area and multiply by a third dimension.

For instance, to find the volume of a rectangular object, you would multiply the length times the width (a.k.a. the area) by the height (the third dimension). So to find the volume of a quadrilateral, the only kind of figure you are likely to see in a volume question, you just use this formula:

length × width × height = volume

For example:

What is the volume of a rectangular fish tank with the following specifications:

length: 6 inches

height: 6 inches

width: 10 inches

There isn't much to it. Just stick the numbers into the formula.

length × width × height = volume

$6 \times 10 \times 6 = 360$

Practice — Area and volume (the answers are on p. 111)

1. If the area of a square is equal to its perimeter, what is the length of one side?

    (A) 1
    (B) 2
    (C) 4
    (D) 8
    (E) 10

2. The area of a rectangle with width 4 and length 3 is equal to the area of a triangle with a base of 6 and a height of

    (F) 1
    (G) 2
    (H) 3
    (J) 4
    (K) 12

3. Two cardboard boxes have equal volume. The dimensions of one box are $3 \times 4 \times 10$. If the length of the other box is 6 and the width is 4, what is the height of the second box?

(A) 2
(B) 5
(C) 10
(D) 12
(E) 24

4. If the area of a square is $64p^2$, what is the length of one side of the square?

(F) $64p^2$
(G) $8p^2$
(H) $64p$
(J) $8p$
(K) 8

CHARTS AND GRAPHS

Charts

Chart questions are simple, but you must be careful. Follow these three steps and you'll be well on your way to mastering any chart question.

1. Read any text that accompanies the chart. It is important to know what the chart is showing and what scale the numbers are on.

2. Read the question.

3. Refer to the chart and find the specific information you need.

If there is more than one question about a single chart, the later questions will tend to be more difficult than the earlier ones. Be careful!

Here is a sample chart of Club membership by state, 1995 and 1996:

State	1995	1996
California	300	500
Florida	225	250
Illinois	200	180
Massachusetts	150	300
Michigan	150	200
New Jersey	200	250
New York	400	600
Texas	50	100

There are lots of different questions that you can answer based on the information in this chart. For instance:

What is the difference between the number of members who came from New York in 1995 and the number of members who came from Illinois in 1996?

This question asks you to look up two simple pieces of information and then do a tiny bit of math. First, the number of members who came from New York in 1995 was 400. Second, the number of members who came from Illinois in 1996 was 180. Finally, look back at the question. It asks you to find the difference between these numbers. 400 – 180 = 220. Done.

What was the percent increase in members from New Jersey from 1995 to 1996?

You should definitely know how to do this one. Do you remember how to translate percentage questions? If not, go back to the section on percentages!

In 1995, there were 200 club members from New Jersey. In 1996 there were 250 members from New Jersey. That represents an increase of 50 members. So to determine the percent increase, you will need to ask yourself "50 (the increase) is what percent of 200 (the original amount)?"

Translated, this becomes:

$$50 = \frac{g}{100} \times 200$$

With a little bit of simple manipulation, this equation becomes:

$$50 = 2g$$

. . . and . . .

$$25 = g$$

So from 1995 to 1996, there was a 25 percent increase in the number of members from New Jersey. Good work!

Which state had as many club members in 1996 as a combination of Illinois, Massachusetts, and Michigan had in 1995?

First, take a second to look up the number of members who came from Illinois, Massachusetts, and Michigan in 1995 and add them together.

$$200 + 150 + 150 = 500$$

Which state had 500 members in 1996? California. That's all there is to it!

Graphs

Some questions will ask you to interpret a graph. You should be familiar with both pie and bar graphs. These graphs are generally drawn to scale (meaning that the graphs give an accurate visual impression of the information) so you can always guess based on the figure if you need to.

The way to approach a graph question is exactly the same as the way to approach a chart question. Follow the same three steps:

1. Read any text that accompanies the graph. It is important to know what the graph is showing and what scale the numbers are on.

2. Read the question.

3. Refer back to the graph and find the specific information you need.

This is how it works:

Figure 1

The graph in Figure 1 shows Emily's clothing expenditures for the month of October. On which type of clothing did she spend the most money?

(A) Shoes
(B) Shirts
(C) Socks
(D) Hats
(E) Pants

This one is easy. You can look at the pieces of the pie and identify the largest, or you can look at the amounts shown in the graph and choose the largest one. Either way, the answer is (A), because Emily spent more money on shoes than on any other clothing items in October.

Emily spent half of her clothing money on which two items?

(A) Shoes and pants
(B) Shoes and shirts
(C) Hats and socks
(D) Socks and shirts
(E) Shirts and pants

Again, you can find the answer to this question two different ways. You can look for which two items together make up half the chart, or you can add up the total amount of money Emily spent ($240) and then figure out which two items made up half (or $120) of that amount. Either way is just fine, and either way, the right answer is (B), shoes and shirts.

Practice — Chart and graph problems (the answers are on p. 111)

Questions 1–3 refer to the following summary of energy costs by district

District	1990	1991
A	400	600
B	500	700
C	200	350
D	100	150
E	600	800

(all numbers are in thousands of dollars)

1. In 1991, which district spent twice as much on energy as district A spent in 1990?

   (A) A
   (B) B
   (C) C
   (D) D
   (E) E

2. Which district spent the most on electricity in 1990 and 1991 combined?

   (F) A
   (G) B
   (H) D
   (J) E
   (K) It cannot be determined from the information given.

3. The total increase in energy expenditure in these districts, from 1990 to 1991, is how many dollars?

   (A) $800
   (B) $1,800
   (C) $2,400
   (D) $2,600
   (E) $800,000

Questions 4–5 refer to Figure 2, which shows the number of compact discs owned by five students.

Figure 2

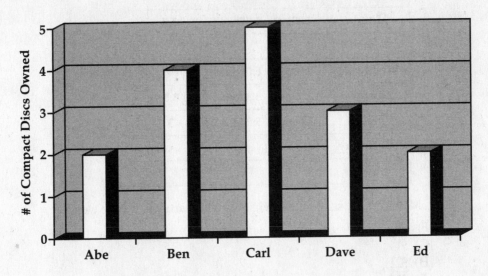

4. Carl owns as many CDs as which two other students combined?

   (F) Abe and Ben
   (G) Ben and Dave
   (H) Abe and Ed
   (J) Abe and Dave
   (K) Ben and Ed

5. Which one student owns one-fourth of the CDs accounted for in Figure 2?

   (A) Abe
   (B) Ben
   (C) Carl
   (D) Dave
   (E) Ed

Questions 6–8 refer to Matt's weekly time card shown below.

Day	In	Out	Hours Worked
Monday	2:00pm	5:30pm	3.5
Tuesday			
Wednesday	2:00pm	6:00pm	4
Thursday	2:00pm	5:30pm	3.5
Friday	2:00pm	5:00pm	3
Saturday			
Sunday			

6. If Matt's hourly salary is $6, what were his earnings for the week?

   (F) $6
   (G) $14
   (H) $21
   (J) $54
   (K) $84

7. What is the average number of hours Matt worked on the days he worked during this particular week?

   (A) 3
   (B) 3.5
   (C) 4
   (D) 7
   (E) 14

8. The hours that Matt worked on Monday accounted for what percent of the total number of hours he worked during this week?

   (F) 3.5
   (G) 20
   (H) 25
   (J) 35
   (K) 50

MATH REVIEW

Make sure you can confidently answer all of the following questions before you take the SHSAT. (The answers are on p. 112)

1. Is zero an integer? _____

2. Is zero positive or negative? _____

3. What operation do you perform to find a sum? _____

4. What operation do you perform to find a product? _____

5. What is the result called when you divide?_____

6. Is 312 divisible by 3?_____
   Is 312 divisible by 9? _____
   (Actually dividing isn't fair—use your divisibility rules!)

7. What does the "E" in PEMDAS stand for?_____

8. Is 3 a factor of 12? Is 12 a factor of 3?_____

9. Is 3 a multiple of 12? Is 12 a multiple of 3?_____

10. What is the tens digit in the number 304.275?_____

11. What is the tenths digit in the number 304.275? _____

12. 2^3 =_____

13. In "math language" the word "percent" means: _____

14. In "math language" the word "of" means:_____

15. In a ratio box, the last column on the right is always the _____.

16. Whenever you see a problem involving averages, draw the _____.

17. When a problem contains variables in the question and in the answers, I will
    _____.

18. To find the perimeter of a square, _____ the length(s) of _____ side(s).

19. To find the area of a square, _____ the length(s) of _____ sides(s).

20. There are _____ degrees in a straight line.

21. A triangle has _____ angles which total degrees.

22. A four-sided figure contains _____ degrees.

23. An isosceles triangle has _____ equal sides; an _____ triangle has three equal sides.

24. The longest side of a right triangle is called the _____ and is located opposite the _____.

25. To find the area of a triangle, use the formula: _____.

5

SHSAT Verbal

INTRODUCTION

The Verbal section on the SHSAT consists of:

- 5 scrambled paragraphs (worth two questions each)

- 10 logical reasoning questions

- 30 reading comprehension questions

That's 45 questions, but you only have 75 minutes! Should you try to spend 90 seconds on each question to get them all done? *No!*

YOU MEAN I DON'T HAVE TO DO ALL THE QUESTIONS?

Nope. You'll actually improve your score by answering fewer questions, as long as you're still using all of the allotted time.

Why rush through questions you can get right if you are careful, to get to the really tough ones that almost no one gets? That approach only ensures that you will make hasty, careless errors. Work as slowly as you need to on the questions you know you can do, to make sure you get them right. Then try the harder ones.

Look at Chapter 2 to see how many verbal questions you need to complete in order to reach your target score. Pace yourself—you'll have much more time for each question than the students who think they have to get them all done.

WHICH QUESTIONS SHOULD I DO?

The questions are arranged roughly in order of difficulty—the harder questions tend to come toward the end of each section.

However, everyone is different. You'll know some questions that your friends won't, and vice versa. What makes some verbal questions difficult is different for each person.

You get as many points for an easy question as you do for a hard one. *So do all the questions that are easy for you first.* Then go back through and do the ones you sort of know. You'll probably be staying mostly in the beginning and middle of each section, but don't be afraid to glance ahead—there may be some questions that will be easy for you toward the end. (Remember to skip a number on the answer sheet when you skip a question!)

THE PROCESS OF ELIMINATION

POE is the key to getting verbal questions right. With math questions, there's always a correct answer, and the other answers are simply wrong. In a verbal question, however, things are not that simple. Words are a lot more slippery than numbers. So verbal questions have "best" answers, not necessarily "correct" answers. The other answers aren't necessarily wrong, but the SHSAT thinks they're not as good as the "best" one. This means that your goal is to eliminate "worse" answer choices in the verbal and reading sections.

Get used to looking for "worse" answers. There are a lot more of them than there are "best" answers, so "worse" answers are easier to find! When you find them, cross them out in the question booklet. No matter which other techniques you use to answer a question, you should always be eliminating wrong answers, instead of trying to magically pick out the best answer.

One thing to remember for the Verbal section: You cannot eliminate answer choices that contain words you don't know or don't understand. Just because you don't understand it, doesn't mean it's the wrong answer.

WHAT IF I CAN'T NARROW IT DOWN TO ONE ANSWER?

Should you guess? Yes. If you can't eliminate even one answer choice, you should guess.

WHERE DO I START?

In the Verbal section, do the reading comprehension questions first—they're the most plentiful, and you need to get a large number of them correct in order to get a good score.

You'll be taking two passes over each section, moving through the sections in this order:

1. Reading comprehension
2. Logical reasoning
3. Scrambled paragraphs

PACING AND VERBAL STRATEGY

Take a look at the pacing advice in Chapter 3 to help answer the next three questions.

How many reading comprehension questions do I need to do?

How many logical reasoning questions do I need to do?

How many scrambled paragraphs do I need to do?

When I start the verbal section, what question number do I start on?

What's the order in which I do questions in the verbal section?

      1.

      2.

      3.

What's the technique I'll be using all the time, regardless of whatever else I'm using to answer a question?

How many answer choices must I have eliminated in order to guess productively?

Can I eliminate answer choices that contain words I don't know?

If you have trouble answering any of the questions above, reread this chapter!

READING

WHAT'S READING ALL ABOUT ON THE SHSAT?

You have to read the SHSAT reading passages differently from the way you would read anything else, because the passages the test writers use are dense with information. Generally, when you read a textbook or any other book, you might notice one or two phrases you want to remember in each paragraph. On the SHSAT, however, the passages are chosen precisely because they give a lot of information in only a few paragraphs. It's all packed in together. So if you read the normal way, here's what happens: You read the first sentence and you try to remember it. You read the second sentence and try to remember it. You read the third sentence and, as you try to remember it, you forget the first two.

You have to read with a different goal in mind for the SHSAT. This may sound crazy, but *don't* try to learn or remember anything. *You don't get any points for reading the passage well!*

What do you get points for? Answering questions correctly. On the questions and answers, you need to slow down and make sure you're checking each answer carefully before eliminating it. Don't worry about finishing the section, those that do are probably hurting their scores as they rush through the questions.

WHAT ARE THE PASSAGES LIKE?

There are five reading passages with six questions each in the Verbal section.

You should be selective as you work through the passages. Don't let the test writers choose which ones you'll get to. Flip through them and go with the questions that center on topics that interest you (if there are any!).

Which types of passages do you do better on? You will learn this as you do practice questions and practice SHSATs.

Passage types

The history and science passages sound like parts of textbooks—they tend to be unemotional and objective. The parts of a story or actual historical documents can be disorienting in comparison, because often you will get no warning as to who is speaking or writing, or into what time or place you've been dropped. You need to get as much of that information as possible from the clues in the passage. Of course, the poems are open to even more interpretation—make sure you do well on the practice poem passages if you plan on attempting them on the test.

HOW DO I READ THE PASSAGES?

Quickly! Don't try to remember the details in the passage. Your goal is to read the passage quickly to get the main idea.

The SHSAT Reading Comprehension section is like an open-book test—you can look back at the passage to answer specific questions.

Label the paragraphs

After you read each paragraph, ask yourself what you just read. Put it in your own words—as briefly as you can—and write your summary at the side of the paragraph. This way you'll have something to guide you back to the relevant part of the passage when you have to answer a question.

You need to be able to go back to the passage and find the answer to a question quickly. You don't want to have to look through every paragraph to find it! The key to labeling the paragraphs is practice; you need to do it quickly, coming up with one or two words that accurately remind you of what's in the paragraph.

If the passage has only one paragraph, try stopping every few sentences to label them with a word or two. Stories, excerpts from diaries, and poems do not need to be labeled.

State the main idea

After you have read the entire passage, ask yourself two questions:

- "What?"— What is the passage about?

- "So what?"— What's the author's point about this topic?

The answers to these questions will show you the main idea of the passage. Scribble down this main idea in just a few words. The answer to "What?" is the thing that was being talked about—bees, for instance. The answer to "So what?" gives you the rest of the sentence: Bees do little dances that tell other bees where to go for pollen.

Don't assume you will find the main idea in the first paragraph. While often the main idea is in the beginning of the passage, it is not *always* in the first sentence or even the first paragraph. The beginning may just be a lead-in to the main point.

Practice—Getting through the passage (the answers are on p. 113)

As you quickly read each paragraph, label it. When you finish the passage, answer "What?" and "So what?" to get the main idea.

Contrary to popular belief, the first European known to lay eyes on America was not Christopher Columbus or Amerigo Vespucci, but a little-known Viking named Bjarni Herjolfsson. In the summer of 986, Bjarni sailed from Norway to Iceland, heading for the Viking settlement where his father Heriulf resided.

When he arrived in Iceland, Bjarni discovered that his father had already sold his land and estates and set out for the latest Viking settlement on the subarctic island called Greenland. Discovered by a notorious murderer and criminal named Eric the Red, Greenland lay at the limit of the known world. Dismayed, Bjarni set out for this new colony.

Since the Vikings traveled without a chart or compass, it was not uncommon for them to lose their way in the unpredictable northern seas. Beset by fog, the crew lost their bearings. When the fog finally cleared, they found themselves before a land that was level and covered with woods.

They traveled farther up the coast, finding more flat, wooded country. Farther north, the landscape revealed glaciers and rocky mountains. Though Bjarni realized this was an unknown land, he was no intrepid explorer. Rather, he was a practical man who had simply set out to find his father. Refusing his crew's request to go ashore, he promptly turned his bow back out to sea. After four days' sailing, Bjarni landed at Herjolfsnes on the southwestern tip of Greenland, the exact place he had been seeking all along.

"What" is this passage about?

"So what?" What's the author's point?

What type of passage is this?

THE QUESTIONS

Now we're getting to the important part of the Reading Comprehension section. This is where you need to spend time in order to avoid careless errors. After reading a passage, you'll see a group of questions that are in no particular order. The first thing you need to decide is whether the question you're answering is general or specific.

General questions

General questions are about the passage as a whole. There are five types:

Main Idea

- Which of the following best tells what this passage is about?

- The passage is primarily about

- The main idea of the passage is

- The best title for this passage would be

Tone/Attitude

- The author's tone is

- The attitude of the author is one of

General Interpretation

- The author's tone/attitude indicates

- Which of these statements would the author most likely agree with?

- This passage deals with X by

- The passage implies that

- Which of the following words best describes the passage?

- It can be inferred from the passage that

- The style of the passage is

- Where would you be likely to find this passage?

- What is the author's opinion of X?

- The passage is best described as a

Purpose

- The purpose of the passage is

- The author wrote this passage in order to

Prediction

- Which is likely to happen next?

- The author will most likely discuss *X* next.

Notice that all of these questions require that you know the main idea, but the ones at the end of the list require you to do a little more interpreting.

Answering a general question

Keep your answers to "What? So what?" in mind. The answer to a general question will somehow pertain to the main idea. If you need details, go back to your paragraph labels. The labels will allow you to quickly hone in on the details you need.

- For a straight **main idea** question, just ask yourself, "What was the 'What? So what?' for this passage?"

- For a **tone/attitude question**, ask yourself, "How did the author feel about the subject?"

- For a **general interpretation** question, ask yourself, "Which answer sounds most like what the author said and how he said it?"

- For a **general purpose** question, ask yourself, "Why did the author write this?"

- For a **prediction** question, ask yourself, "How was the passage arranged?" Take a quick look at your paragraph labels.

Answer the question in your own words before looking at the answer choices. As always, you want to arm yourself with your own answer before looking at the SHSAT's tricky answers.

Practice — Answering a general question (the answers are on p. 113)

Take a look at the passage about Vikings that you just read and labeled. Reread your main idea and answer the following questions. Use the questions above to help you paraphrase your own answer before looking at the choices.

1. Which of the following best tells what this passage is about?
   (A) the Vikings and their civilization
   (B) the waves of Viking immigration
   (C) sailing techniques of Bjarni Herjolfsson
   (D) one Viking's glimpse of the new world
   (E) the hazards of Viking travel

2. With which of the following statements about Viking explorers would the author most probably agree?

   (F) Greenland and Iceland were the Vikings' final discoveries.

   (G) Viking explorers were cruel and savage.

   (H) The Vikings' most startling discovery was an accidental one.

   (J) Bjarni Herjolfsson was the first settler of America.

   (K) All Viking explorers were fearless.

3. What was the author's purpose in writing this passage?

   (A) to turn the reader against Italian adventurers

   (B) to show his disdain for Eric the Red

   (C) to demonstrate the Vikings' nautical skills

   (D) to correct a common misconception about the European discovery of America

   (E) to prove the Vikings were far more advanced than previously thought

Specific questions

Specific questions are about a detail or a section of the passage. There are four main types:

1. Fact

- According to the passage/author

- The author states that

- Which of these questions is answered by the passage?

- Which of the following is **not** mentioned in the passage?

2. Definition in Context

- What does the passage mean by X?

- X probably represents/means

- Which word best replaces the word X without changing the meaning?

3. Specific Interpretation

- The author implies, in line X

- It can be inferred from paragraph X

- The most likely interpretation of X is

4. Purpose

- The author uses *X* in order to

- Why does the author say *X*?

Like the general questions, the questions above range from flat-out requests for information found in the passage to questions that require some interpretation of the information in the passage.

Answering a specific question

For specific questions, always reread the relevant part of the passage. Remember, this is an open-book test!
   To find the relevant part:

- Use your **paragraph labels** to go straight to the information you need.

- Use the **line or paragraph reference**, if there is one, but be careful. With a line reference, be sure to read five lines before and five lines after, not just the referenced line. For instance, if the question says "in line 10 . . ." you need to read lines 5 through 15 to actually find the answer.

- You might even want to circle words that stand out in the question and passage, such as names, places, and long words. We call these **lead words** because they lead you back to the right place in the passage.

   Once you're in the right area, answer the question in your own words. Then look at the answer choices and eliminate any that aren't like yours.

Definition-in-context questions

Creating your own answer before looking at the choices makes **definition-in-context** questions especially easy. Remember, they want to know how the word or phrase is being used *in context*, so come up with your own word that fits in the sentence before looking at the answer choices. Try one:

   In line 15, the word "spot" most closely means

Cross out the word they're asking about, and replace it with your own. Here's the section from the passage:

   A raptor must also have a sharp, often hooked beak so that it may tear the flesh of its prey. Because they hunt from the sky, these birds must have extremely sharp eyesight, which allows them to *spot* potential prey from a great distance.

Now look at the answer choices and eliminate the ones that are not at all like yours.

   (A) taint

   (B) mark

   (C) hunt

   (D) detect

   (E) circle

You probably came up with something like "see." The closest answer to "see" is (D). Notice that "taint" and "mark" are possible meanings of "spot," but they don't work in this context. Those answer choices are there to catch students who do not go back to the passage to see how the word is used.

Definition-in-context questions are so quick to answer that if you only have a little time left, you should definitely spend it working on them.

I, II, III questions

The questions that have three roman numerals can be confusing and relatively time-consuming. They look like this:

According to the passage, which of the following is true?

    I. The sky is blue.

   II. Nothing rhymes with "orange."

  III. Smoking cigarettes increases lung capacity.

        (A) I only

        (B) II only

        (C) III only

        (D) I and II only

        (E) I, II, and III

For these questions, you'll need to look up each of the three statements in the passage; it's important to make sure that you look up just one statement at a time.

For instance, in the question above, say you look back at the passage and see that the passage says statement I is true. Write a big "T" next to it. What can you eliminate? Answers (B) and (C). Now you check out II, and you find that sure enough, they've said that, too. So II gets a big "T" and you cross off answer (A). Next, while looking in the paragraph you labeled "Smoking is bad," you find that the passage actually says that smoking decreases lung capacity. What can you eliminate? Answer (E).

You may need to skip a **I, II, III** question because it will be too time-consuming, especially if you're on your last reading passage and there are other questions you can do instead.

Except/Least/Not questions

This is another confusing type of question. The test writers are reversing what you need to look for by asking you which answer is false.

Which of the following can **not** be inferred from the passage?

Before you go any further, cross out the "**not.**" Now you have a "positive" question to answer. Of course, as always, you will go through *all* the answer choices, but for this type of question you will put a little "Y" or "N" next to the answers as you check them out. Let's say these are the answer choices:

        (A) Americans are patriotic.   **Y**

        (B) Americans have great ingenuity.   **Y**

        (C) Americans love war.   **N**

        (D) Americans do what they can to help

            one another.   **Y**

        (E) Americans are brave in times of war. **Y**

Which one stands out? The one with the "N." That's your answer. You made a confusing question much simpler than the test writers wanted it.

You should skip an except/least/not question if you're on your last passage and there are other questions you can do instead.

Practice—Answering a specific question (the answers are on p. 113)

Answer the following questions using the passage about Vikings that you just read and labeled. Use your paragraph labels and the lead words in each question to get to the part of the passage you need, and put the answer in your own words before looking at the answer choices.

1. According to the passage, Bjarni Herjolfsson left Norway to

   (A) found a new colony.

   (B) open trading lanes.

   (C) visit his relatives.

   (D) map the North Sea.

   (E) settle in Greenland.

2. Bjarni's reaction upon landing in Iceland can best be described as

   (F) disappointed.

   (G) satisfied.

   (H) amused.

   (J) indifferent.

   (K) fascinated.

3. "The crew lost their bearings," in the third paragraph, probably means that

   (A) the ship was damaged beyond repair.

   (B) the crew became disoriented.

   (C) the crew decided to mutiny.

   (D) the crew went insane.

   (E) the ship's compass broke.

4. It can be inferred from the passage that prior to Bjarni Herjolfsson's voyage, Greenland

   (F) was covered in grass and shrubs.

   (G) was overrun with Vikings.

   (H) was rich in fish and game.

   (J) was populated by criminals.

   (K) was as far west as the Vikings had traveled.

Before you even look at the answer choices, come up with your own answer, in your own words. What do you do next?

Well, you're looking for the answer that's closest to yours, but it's a lot easier to eliminate answers than to try to magically zone in on the "best" one. Work through the answers using process of elimination. As soon as you eliminate an answer, cross off the letter in your test booklet so it doesn't confuse you.

How Can I Eliminate Answer Choices?

On a general question
Avoid answers that

- are too detailed. The passage may mention it, but it's only a detail, not a main idea.

- are not mentioned in the passage.

- are in contradiction to the passage. It might say the opposite of what you read.

- are too big. The answer tries to say that more was discussed or proved than really was. The passages consist of only a few short paragraphs. Not many things can be definitively proven in only a few short paragraphs. Broad topics or complicated subjects are often not the correct answers.

- are too extreme. An extreme answer is too negative or too positive, or it uses absolute words like "all," "every," "never," or "always." If you have two answers that express a similar idea, there's a good chance that the one that's stated firmly is probably wrong, while the other, more moderate one, is probably correct. Eliminating extreme answers makes tone/attitude questions much easier.

- go against common sense. The passage is not likely to back up answers that don't make sense at all.

On a specific question
Avoid answers that

- are extreme.

- contradict passage details.

- are not mentioned in the passage.

- are direct quotes. If it contains a few words that are written exactly as they appeared in the passage there's a good chance that it's a trap. An answer that says the same thing as the passage did, but in slightly different words (a paraphrase) would be better.

- go against common sense.

If you look back at the questions you did for the Viking passage, you'll see that many of the wrong answer choices fit into the categories above.

What kinds of answers do I keep?

"Best" answers are likely to be

- paraphrases of the words in the passage.
- traditional and conservative in their outlook.
- moderate, using words like "may," "can," and "often."

Practice — Eliminating answers (the answers are on pp. 113–114)

The following phrases are answer choices. You haven't read the passage, or even the question, that goes with each of them. However, you *can* decide if each one is a *possible* correct answer, based on the criteria we just listed. Cross out any that you can eliminate.

For a General Question

(A) The author refutes each argument exhaustively.

(B) The author admires the courage of most Americans.

(C) Creativity finds full expression in a state of anarchy.

(D) The passage criticizes Western society for not allowing freedom of expression to artists.

(E) The ancient Egyptians were barbaric.

(F) The author proves that Native American writing does not have a multicultural perspective.

(G) The author emphasizes the significance of diversity in the United States.

(H) The passage reports the record cold temperatures in Boston in 1816.

For a General Tone/Attitude Question

(I) respectful

(J) confused

(K) angry condemnation

(L) admiring

(M) mournful

(N) objective

(O) thrilled optimism

(P) exaggeration

(Q) disgusted

(R) neutral

(S) condescending

(T) indifferent

For a Specific Question

(U) They were always in danger of being deprived of their power.

(V) Voters were easily misled by mud-slinging campaigns.

(W) One-celled organisms act in fairly predictable ways.

(X) Only a show of athletic ability can excite an audience.

(Y) Economic events can have political repercussions.

When you've got it down to two

If you've eliminated all but two answers, don't get stuck and waste time. Keep the main idea in the back of your mind, step back, and follow these steps:

1. Reread the question.

2. Look at what makes the two answers different.

3. Go back to the passage.

4. Ask yourself which answer is worse, and eliminate it.

THE READING PLAN

THE PASSAGES

After I read each paragraph, I _____ it.

After I read an entire passage, I ask myself _____ ? _____?

I am better at doing these types of passages:

THE QUESTIONS

The five main types of general questions, and the questions I can ask myself in order to answer them, are:

_____   _____

_____   _____

_____   _____

_____   _____

To find the answer to a specific question, I can use three clues:

_____

_____

_____

If the question says "in line 22," where do I begin reading for the answer?

_____

_____

_____

_____

The Answers

On a general question, I eliminate answers that are:

_____

_____

_____

_____

On a specific question, I eliminate answers that are:

_____

_____

_____

_____

_____

When I've got it down to two possible answers, I:

_____

_____

_____

_____

If you have trouble answering any of these questions, be sure to reread this chapter before moving on.

Practice — All reading techniques (the answers are on p. 114)

The term "tides" has come to represent the cyclical rising and falling of ocean waters, most notably along the shoreline as the border between land and sea moves in and out throughout the day. The primary reason for this constant redefinition of the sea's boundaries is the gravitational force of the Moon.

The force of lunar gravity is not as strong as Earth's own gravitational pull, which keeps our bodies and our homes from being pulled off the ground, through the sky, and into space toward the Moon. It is a strong enough force, however, to exert a certain gravitational pull as the Moon passes over the Earth's surface. This pull causes the water level to rise (as the water is literally pulled ever-so-slightly toward the Moon) in those parts of the ocean that are exposed to the Moon and its gravitational forces. When the water level in one part of the ocean rises, it naturally must fall in another, and this is what causes water level to change, dramatically at times, along any given piece of coastline.

1. Which one of the following is the most obvious effect of the tides?

   (A) A part of the beach that was once dry is now underwater.

   (B) Floods cause great damage during heavy rainstorms.

   (C) The moon is not visible.

   (D) Water falls.

   (E) The ocean rises.

2. The word "lunar" in the beginning of the second paragraph most nearly means

   (F) weak.

   (G) strong.

   (H) destructive.

   (J) related to the Moon.

   (K) foolish.

3. It can be inferred from the passage that if one were to travel to the Moon

   (A) water would be found on its surface.

   (B) an object, if dropped, would float away from the surface of the Moon.

   (C) other planets besides the Moon have an influence on the tides of the Earth's oceans.

   (D) tides are more dramatic during the day than during the night.

   (E) an object, if dropped, would fall to the Moon's surface.

4. The author's primary purpose in writing this passage is to

   (F) prove the existence of water on the Moon.

   (G) refute claims that tides are caused by the Moon.

   (H) explain the main cause of the ocean's tides.

   (J) argue that humans should not interfere with the processes of nature.

   (K) convince students to study astrophysics.

Additional practice

Read the editorial pages and the science section of a major newspaper to get practice reading short passages with lots of information in them. For even more reading passages and questions (some of which will be harder than SHSAT passages), check out the book *10 Real SATs*, which is published by the College Board.

LOGICAL REASONING

WHAT IS A LOGICAL REASONING QUESTION?

It's just a word puzzle! There are 10 logical reasoning questions on the SHSAT. They may sound complicated, but they're actually simple riddles that can be fun! From now on we'll refer to these questions as games.

The best way to play these games is to draw pictures of them. You should never try to figure out the games in your head; writing them out is the way to go. Different types of games require different types of pictures to keep track of the information. With a little practice you should have no trouble deciding what type of picture to draw for each game.

DRAW THE GAMES

First the game will give you some information. For instance:

A pie contains three types of fruit.

It will then list some conditions. These conditions are the rules of the game. They tell you what can and cannot be done. For instance:

There are five types of fruit that can be used in the pie: apples, bananas, cherries, plums, and oranges. Cherries and plums must be used together.

Then you will be asked a question regarding the information. The questions usually have to do with relationships—they ask who is taller or shorter or heavier or lighter, where something can be (top or bottom, left or right, over or under), or what kinds of combinations can be made. These questions can be easily answered if you remember all the conditions. The best way to do this is by symbolizing them. Let's see how to do this.

USING SYMBOLS

SET-UP	SYMBOL

There are five types of fruit—apples, bananas, cherries, plums, and oranges. Cherries and plums must be used together.

Let's symbolize the information so we can work with it. Lets write out "a, b, c, p, o" and put c and p in a block: [c p]. Now we can answer the question more easily.

Which of the following fruits can be used together in a pie?

(A) apples, bananas, and plums
(B) plums, cherries, and bananas
(C) bananas, cherries, and apples
(D) bananas, cherries, and oranges
(E) apples, plums, and oranges

Answer (A) doesn't have c and p together; neither do (C), (D), or (E), so our answer must be (B), the only answer that follows the rule.

Remember that all the information you need is in the question. You don't need any special knowledge to solve these problems, but you do have to "play the game" to find the answers.

Make sure that you use *all* the information they give you when you make a drawing or symbol, and don't add any information that isn't provided.

So, if a game says that Joe is "behind" Bob, that doesn't mean he's directly behind Bob. Someone else could also be behind Bob and ahead of Joe. A good way to symbolize this would be B...J. This indicates their positions in relation to each other, and allows for the fact that other people could be between them. Be careful—not reading carefully and not using symbols accurately are both common mistakes.

Examples

For each of the words or phrases below, we have drawn a picture or a symbol.

Make symbols as clear as possible. Three chairs, for example, are best symbolized as "c c c" rather than "3 c's."

SETUP	SYMBOL
1. B stands between A and C.	A...B...C or C...B...A
2. A bag contains ten marbles: yellow, blue, and green. The number of blue marbles is less than or equal to the number of yellow marbles.	$y + b + g = 10$ $b \leq y$
3. Tom and George never work together.	$T \neq G$
4. A, B, and C are juniors; D, E, and F are seniors.	$A_J B_J C_J$ $D_S E_S F_S$
5. A certain class has four girls and three boys.	gggg bbb
6. On a certain shelf are three French books and two Spanish books. The French books are next to each other. The Spanish books are not next to each other.	FFF $\boxed{s\!\!\!/\,s}$
7. In a six-story hotel, Q lives two floors above R.	$\boxed{\begin{array}{c} Q \\ \hline R \end{array}}$
8. If Bill plays first, Tom plays second.	$B_1 \rightarrow T_2$
9. In a marathon, G finishes before H, H finishes before I, and J finishes before I.	G...H...I...J

Let's take a look at another game, and write clear symbols for each clue.

Questions numbered 1–3 refer to the following information:

Five hats are on display in a window. They are numbered consecutively from left to right.

1. One hat is a baseball cap.

2. The top hat is fourth from the left.

3. There are exactly 3 hats between the fedora and coonskin cap.

4. There are exactly 2 hats to the left of the helmet; one of them is the fedora.

With this question, we actually get our first piece of information in the question itself: We know there are five hats. Let's draw that:

__	__	__	__	__
1	2	3	4	5

Our first clue tells us there is a baseball cap, which we'll call B. The second clue tells us there is a top-hat, T, in the fourth slot, let's draw that like this:

__	__	__	T	__
1	2	3	4	5

The third clue tells us there are three slots between the F and the C. The only arrangement that allows for this is:

F or C	__	__	T	C or F
1	2	3	4	5

But we still don't know which one comes first and which comes fifth.

The fourth clue actually tells us two things: that the H is in the third slot, and that the F is in one of the two spaces to the left of it.

(F)	(F)	H	T	__
1	2	3	4	5

Now we can put all of these together. If we look at the last two clues, we know that the F has to be in 1, the H is in 3, and the C is in 5.

F	__	H	T	C
1	2	3	4	5

Now we're almost done. The only hat left is the B, which must go in 2.

F	B	H	T	C
1	2	3	4	5

With our completed diagram we can answer the questions with ease.

1. In which position is the baseball cap?
   (A) second
   (B) third
   (C) fourth
   (D) fifth
   (E) It cannot be determined from the information given.

It's easy to select (A) as the correct answer, thanks to all our work. Let's look at the next question.

2. Which hat is farthest to the left?

   (F) top hat
   (G) fedora
   (H) coonskin cap
   (J) helmet
   (K) It cannot be determined from the information given.

Once again it's a breeze to select the correct answer, (G).
One more question to go.

3. What hat is located 2 spots to the right of the baseball cap?

   (A) helmet
   (B) coonskin cap
   (C) fedora
   (D) top hat
   (E) It cannot be determined from the information given.

Lo and behold, once again it's easy. Starting at the B and counting over two slots, we see we have the T, which is answer (D).

By being careful, symbolizing our clues and writing everything down, we were able to get the answers to all three questions fairly easily.

Now let's move on to another type of game.

CODE GAMES

There will probably be at least one logical reasoning question that deals with codes. You will be asked to determine what certain parts of a code stand for, or how to write something in a code. The most important thing to know about these games is that *the code symbols will not be in the same order as the items they represent.*

For example:

In the code that follows, each punctuation mark stands for one syllable in the name of each town.

* –	means	"Norfolk"
& –	means	"Norwood"
& !	means	"Woodglen"
: !	means	"Glenhill"
: @	means	"Hillcrest"
/ @	means	"Crestdale"

1. What symbols are needed to write the name of the town "Crestwood" in code?

   (A) @ !
   (B) : /
   (C) – /
   (D) & @
   (E) * :

The question above asks you how to write "Crestwood." To get an answer, you don't have to know what every part of the code stands for. Just take the question apart piece by piece.

What is the code symbol for "crest"? How do you know? Well, we see that : @ is "Hillcrest" and / @ is "Crestdale." Since @ is in both, it must represent "crest."

Let's use the same approach to determine the symbol for "wood." We see that & – means "Norwood" and that & ! means "Woodglen." Since & is in both, it must represent "wood."

When you look for the answer, remember that the symbols don't have to be in any particular order. Our answer, therefore, must include @ and & in either order. This leads us to answer (D).

Now let's move on to another type of game.

TRUTH GAMES

These games generally involve less drawing. They usually ask you to answer a common-sense question about a fact that *must be true* from the information given. In solving these problems, it is important to *avoid answer choices that introduce new information.*

In the game below, eliminate all choices that do not have to be true from the information given.

> Trixie goes to college three days a week, and she works two days a week. Trixie never works on the same days she goes to school.
>
> If all of the information above is true, which of the following must also be true?
>
> (A) Trixie spends more time at school than she does at work.
> (B) Trixie always has her weekends free.
> (C) No one can both go to school and work on the same day.
> (D) On exactly two days per week, Trixie does not work or go to college.
> (E) Trixie uses the money she earns to put herself through college.

Let's examine each answer choice and see what we know about it.

Answer (A) says Trixie spends more *time* at school than at work, but what the original information told us was that she spends more *days* at school than work. We don't know how many hours per day she spends at either place.

Answer (B) says Trixie's weekends are free. Although we know about her activities on five days of the week, we don't know *which* days these are. She could be working or going to classes on the weekend.

We don't know about answer (C), since it says "no one," and the only person we know about is Trixie.

Answer (D) says we know Trixie isn't in school or working two days a week. This we *do* know, since she doesn't work and go to school on the same day.

Answer (E) introduces new information we know nothing about; we have no idea what she uses her money for.

These games will try to confuse you by putting in choices that *sound* logical, but really aren't. Make sure you stick close to the information you're given. If an answer choice is not absolutely true, get rid of it.

Time to move on to yet another game.

CONCLUSION GAMES

Sometimes you will be asked to pick the setup that would make a statement true. The question might ask "Which of the following leads to the above conclusion?" or "Which makes the above statement valid?" You have to choose the option that would make the statement true.

Let's try it:

One fine morning, in the tiny town of El Diablo on the Texas-Mexico border, Mr. Earle notices Mr. Van Zandt strolling down the avenue with a brand new Martin D-2f acoustic guitar. Mr. Earle concludes that Mr. Van Zandt must have stolen the guitar.

Given no other clues, which of the following must be true in order for Mr. Earle's conclusion to be valid?

(F)   No guitar shop within a thousand miles of El Diablo sells the Martin D-2f.

(G)   Mr. Van Zandt does not know how to play a guitar.

(H)   Mr. Van Zandt is a known criminal, and currently on trial for breaking and entering.

(J)   Mr. Van Zandt is constantly without money, to the point where he often steals from Mr. Earle.

(K)   The only way to obtain a Martin D-2f is by stealing it.

Let's look at each of these answers and see if they prove Mr. Earle's conclusion.

Answer (F) doesn't tell us that Mr. Van Zandt had to have stolen the guitar. He could have traveled to buy it or purchased it by mail order.

Answer (G) also doesn't tell us that the guitar must have been stolen by Mr. Van Zandt. As a matter of fact, it doesn't tell us anything about how he acquired it.

Answer (H) tells us he's a criminal and currently on trial for breaking and entering, but we can't determine if he stole *this* guitar. Once again nothing is mentioned about how he might have acquired it.

Answer (J) tells us Mr. Van Zandt has stolen before, but we don't know for certain if he stole *this* time.

Answer (K) tells us that the only way to acquire one of these guitars is to steal it, and since he has one, he must have stolen it. Even though this sounds pretty silly, it's the only answer choice that makes the conclusion true.

Ready? Here comes another fun game to play!

IF . . . THEN GAMES

"If . . . then" games give you a conditional statement. Let's look at a good way to draw these. Let's say you're given the statement *If it rains then the sidewalk is wet.* Symbolize the key words with letters and use an arrow to show which condition leads to which. The arrow must correctly show the direction of the phrase.

$$\text{If } R \rightarrow W$$

What you *can* do to make the statement true is "flip and negate" it. Switch the positions of the elements and put a not or negative "–" sign in front of each of them. For example:

$$\text{If } {-}W \rightarrow {-}R$$

That means that *if the sidewalk is not wet, then it is not raining.* This is true and, in fact, it's the *only* true conclusion you can draw from the original statement. Once again, just switch the order and put a negative "–" in front of each symbol.

If you started with a negative phrase like *If it's not 12:00 then I'm not hungry*, which you can symbolize like this:

$$-12:00 \rightarrow -H$$

just remove the word *not* when you flip and negate them. The sentence will read: *If I'm hungry then it's 12:00*, which you can symbolize like this:

$$H \rightarrow 12:00$$

Now you try it:

A statement says: *If the light is on then my dog is not sleeping.*

How would you symbolize that?

What's the flipped and negated version of this statement?

What does the flipped and negated version say, in words?

So $L \rightarrow -S$ becomes $S \rightarrow -L$, which means *If my dog is sleeping then the light is not on.*

Now try it out on a question:

QUESTIONS

WORK SPACE

If Bill is wearing orange, then it is Thursday afternoon. Right now, it is Wednesday morning.

Which of the following conclusions is most valid according to the information above?

(A)   Bill is wearing orange.
(B)   Bill is not wearing orange.
(C)   Bill is wearing black velvet.
(D)   If Bill is wearing orange, then it is not Thursday afternoon.
(E)   If it is Thursday afternoon, then Bill cannot wear any color in addition to orange.

If you write out $O \rightarrow Th$, and then "flip and negate" that to $-Th \rightarrow -O$, the only answer that follows this is answer (B). So remember on an "if . . . then" game, "flip and negate" is the way to go. You can practice with the problems that begin on the next page.

Practice — Games drill (the answers are on p. 114)

QUESTIONS   WORK SPACE

1. Four juices—apple, orange, grape, and cherry—can be used to make fruit punch. Fruit punch is made by blending three different juices. All of the following combinations of juices could be used **except**:

   (A) orange, grape, apple
   (B) grape, apple, cherry
   (C) grape, cherry, orange
   (D) cherry, orange, apple
   (E) orange, grape, orange

2. In a certain language, *bing konk park* means "small white cat," *konk ling* means "small dog," and *park fu* means "cat litter." Which word means "white"?

   (F) bing
   (G) konk
   (H) park
   (J) ling
   (K) fu

3. A five-story building has floors numbered 1 through 5. Joe lives two floors above Sam and one floor below Pat. If Sam does not live on floor 1, what floor does Joe live on?

   (A) 1
   (B) 2
   (C) 3
   (D) 4
   (E) 5

4. Tracy has a choice of five colors to use in her painting—blue, red, green, pink, and orange. She uses only three colors. Pink cannot be used with either green or blue. Which of the following groups of colors could she use?

   (F) green, blue, orange
   (G) orange, pink, green
   (H) green, red, pink
   (J) red, pink, blue
   (K) green, blue, pink

5. Wally weighs 120 pounds and Theo weighs 180 pounds. Jack is heavier than Wally. How much does Jack weigh?

   (A) 100 lbs.
   (B) 120 lbs.
   (C) 150 lbs.
   (D) 180 lbs.
   (E) Cannot be determined from the information given.

6. If a = 1, b = 2, c = 3, . . . , z = 26, which of the following groups of numbers would spell "fast"?

(F) 6, 1, 19, 20
(G) 6, 2, 19, 20
(H) 7, 1, 18, 19
(J) 6, 1, 20, 30
(K) 6, 1, 6, 1

7. In a four-story toy store, blocks, dolls, games, and puzzles are each on a different floor. Games are one floor above dolls and two floors below puzzles. What is the correct order of floors from top to bottom?

(A) games, blocks, dolls, puzzles
(B) puzzles, games, dolls, blocks
(C) games, dolls, blocks, puzzles
(D) puzzles, dolls, games, blocks
(E) puzzles, blocks, games, dolls

8. Karen visited three friends—Anthony, Louise, and Theresa—on Saturday. She visited Louise first, and then spent two hours with each of her other two friends. According to the information given, which statement must be true?

(F) Karen likes Louise more than she likes Anthony.
(G) From Theresa's house, Karen went to see Louise.
(H) After leaving Louise's house, Karen went immediately to see another friend.
(J) Karen visited Theresa last.
(K) Karen spent the same amount of time with Theresa as with Anthony.

9. Four monkeys, Buddy, Curly, Frank, and Martha are sitting on a fence. Buddy and Frank cannot sit next to each other and Frank and Martha must sit next to each other. Which of the following is a possible order for them to be sitting in?

(A) Buddy, Frank, Martha, Curly
(B) Frank, Curly, Martha, Buddy
(C) Buddy, Curly, Martha, Frank
(D) Martha, Curly, Buddy, Frank
(E) Curly, Buddy, Frank, Martha

10. Casper sees that the sky is red and concludes that someone is playing a trick on him. Which of the following statements, if true, would do the most to make Casper's conclusion valid?

   (F) Nobody ever plays tricks on Casper unless the sky is red.
   (G) There are rarely red skies where Casper lives.
   (H) People play all kinds of tricks on Casper.
   (J) Casper saw someone suspicious doing something to the sky.
   (K) The only time the sky is red is when a trick is being played on Casper.

11. °Δ means "stupid rat"
    $ # means "pretty cow"
    # * means "pretty llama"
    Which of the following is one possible way to say "stupid cow"?

   (A) $ #
   (B) $*
   (C) #
   (D) Δ$
   (E) °Δ

12. If the Moon is made of cheese, then pigs will fly. If a cow can jump over the Moon, then pigs will fly. Based on the information above, which of the following MUST be true?

   (F) If pigs fly, then the Moon is made of cheese and cows can jump over the Moon.
   (G) If pigs fly, then a cow can jump over the Moon.
   (H) If pigs don't fly, then cows cannot jump over the Moon and the Moon is not made of cheese.
   (J) If the Moon is not made of cheese, then pigs won't fly.
   (K) If the Moon is made of cheese, cows can jump over the Moon.

GAMES TECHNIQUES SUMMARY

As soon as you get to a game, figure out what type it is.

1. Draw it. Use symbols to represent as much of the question as possible. When you put things in order, remember to watch out for terms like *above* or *in front of*. Link as many clues together as you can.

2. For Truth games and Conclusion games, draw as much as possible and make sure to stick with the statements you are given.

3. If it's a Code game, remember that the code can be in a different order from the words.

4. For "If . . . then" games, write out the statements you know are true, especially the flipped and negated version of the original statement.

A NOTE ABOUT PACING

More than anything else, this test is long, both in terms of time and in the number of questions. If you find yourself stuck on a mind-boggling game (or anything else, for that matter), skip it and save it for later. If you get back to it, great. If you don't, just take a guess—you've still wisely used your time to answer questions that are easiest for you.

SCRAMBLED PARAGRAPHS

WHAT IS A SCRAMBLED PARAGRAPH?

There are five scrambled paragraphs on the Verbal section, and they're worth two questions each. Each question gives you five sentences out of order, and your job is to reorder the sentences into a logical and grammatically correct paragraph. Rather than having a series of answer choices for each paragraph, the answer sheet will look like this:

Paragraph 1

	Q	R	S	T	U
The first sentence is	Q	R	S	T	U
The second sentence is	Q	R	S	T	U
The third sentence is	Q	R	S	T	U
The fourth sentence is	Q	R	S	T	U
The fifth sentence is	Q	R	S	T	U

There are several aspects of most or all of the sentences of the scrambled paragraphs you'll see that you should pay attention to. They will offer you clues as to the proper arrangement of the sentences.

TRANSITION WORDS AND PHRASES

Transition words and phrases provide connections between sentences.
For example:

> Potatoes are commonly eaten for their good flavor.
> In addition, they are an excellent source of nutrients.

> The obsolete model was designed for maximum speed.
> On the other hand, the new model focuses more on comfort.

Both "on the other hand" and "in addition" are what we call transition phrases. In the first example, the nutritional value of potatoes is *added* to the fact that they are pretty tasty. This tells us that the two sentences are in the correct order. In the second example, the new model is being compared to the older model. Would it make any sense if the second sentence were first? No! Once again, because of the transition phrase, we know that the two phrases are in the correct order.

Some transitions elaborate on an idea in the same direction, while others elaborate in a different direction. In the first example, the potato is said to have both a good taste and be nutritious. The first sentence mentioned one good thing about the potato, and the next sentence mentioned another good thing. However, in the second example, the new model is compared to the old model, and they are found to be different. The old model focused on speed, while the new model focuses on comfort.

Here are some common "same direction" transitions:

> In addition
> Furthermore
> Also
> Too
> And
> Again

Here are some common "different direction" transitions:

> On the other hand
> Except
> But
> However
> On the contrary

Let's see this at work on a couple of questions.

Practice—Transition drill (the answers are on p. 114)

Underline the transition words in the following examples, and say for each whether it is a *same* direction transition or a *different* direction transition:

1. If a field of study adhered to the scientific method, would you consider it a science?

   Q. These processes—hypothesis, experimentation, and conclusion—are all presented assiduously with each detail accurately and meticulously described.

   R. For this reason, many people consider parapsychology—the study of phenomena that cannot be identified in terms of the laws of "common" science—not to be a true science.

   S. However, parapsychologists follow all the methods and mandates of the scientific method.

   T. And so, I again ask, would you consider parapsychology a science?

   U. The scientific method is a series of processes that are used in "common" science.

2. The rickshaw is often associated with the Japanese.

   Q. But, interestingly, it was actually based on an earlier French carriage called the "broutte."

   R. This association stems from the fact that the word *rickshaw* is shortened from the Japanese *jin riki sha*, which means "man-powered carriages."

   S. The person who created this mix of two cultures was probably an American missionary, Jonathan Goble.

   T. From this example, we can see how innovative ideas are born from the merging of three cultures.

   U. Goble commissioned a Japanese artisan to use the "broutte" as a model in making a carriage for his wife.

Which ones did you identify? Check your answers and see how you did.

PRONOUNS

Pronouns are a short way of referring to something or someone that has already been mentioned, either in a previous sentence or earlier in the same sentence.

For example:

Nava got a new pair of shoes for her birthday.
After trying them on, she decided she didn't like them.

We know that "them" refers to the shoes and that "her" and "she" refer to Nava. The pronouns serve as short cuts, of sorts. Think about how awkward and repetitive it would be to write sentences like this:

Nava got a new pair of shoes for Nava's birthday.
After trying the shoes on, Nava decided Nava didn't like the shoes.

When a pronoun is used correctly, it is obvious which noun it is replacing. If there is any ambiguity, then the pronoun has not been used properly.

Here are some commonly used pronouns:

I, me, you, my, she, he, them, us, your, our, we, their, him, her, this, it, that

Practice—Pronoun drill (the answers are on p. 115)

Circle the pronouns in the following examples and jot down to whom or what they refer.

1. If a field of study adhered to the scientific method, would you consider it a science?

   Q. These processes—hypothesis, experimentation, and conclusion—are all presented assiduously with each detail accurately and meticulously described.

   R. For this reason, many people consider parapsychology—the study of phenomena that cannot be identified in terms of the laws of "common" science—not to be a true science.

   S. However, parapsychologists follow all the methods and mandates of the scientific method.

   T. And so, I again ask, would you consider parapsychology a science?

   U. The scientific method is a series of processes that are used in "common" science.

2. The rickshaw is often associated with the Japanese.

   Q. But, interestingly, it was actually based on an earlier French carriage called the "broutte."

   R. This association stems from the fact that the word *rickshaw* is shortened from the Japanese *jin riki sha*, which means "man-powered-carriages."

   S. The person who created this mix of two cultures was probably an American missionary, Jonathan Goble.

   T. From this example, we can see how innovative ideas are born from the merging of three cultures.

   U. Goble commissioned a Japanese artisan to use the "broutte" as a model in making a carriage for his wife.

Which pronouns did you spot? Check your answers and see how you did.

REFERENCES

References are persons, places, or things in a sentence that have already been introduced in a previous sentence.

Suppose you hear someone say: "Rosa does not want that type of food."

What part of the sentence tells you that you walked in on the middle of the conversation? If you'd just walked in, in the middle of that conversation, you'd probably want to ask, "What type of food?" The phrase "that type of food" refers to something that's already been mentioned in the conversation.

On the SHSAT, references are one of the test-writers' ways of telling you how to order the sentences. If the above sentence were part of a scrambled paragraph, you could look for the sentence that introduces the type of food, and you'd know that it came before the sentence shown above.

References can be divided into two categories: **detail references** and **name references.**

Detail references include references to words, phrases, events, places, or any specific detail that has been presented in a previous sentence. Remember, *a word, phrase, event, place or specific detail cannot be discussed in a paragraph until it is introduced.*

For example:

> The largest Eskimo settlement ever discovered is the Ipiutak site in Alaska.
> The Ipiutak site dates from A.D. 300 and includes a three-mile-long cemetery.

In the example above, the Ipiutak site is introduced in the first sentence and, in the second sentence, details about the site are mentioned.

Once a subject is introduced and defined, it is common to find a paraphrase of the subject in the next sentence. Paraphrasing is a restatement that uses different words.

For example:

> His most famous painting is full of slight shifts in color, texture, and form.
> These variations are what make the painting so appealing.

The artist's shifts in color, texture, and form are introduced in the first sentence. In this context, another way to say "shift" is "variation." Although the author uses a different word, the phrase in the second sentence is a paraphrase of the first sentence.

A **name reference** is a reference to a specific person that has been introduced in a previous sentence. *A sentence cannot discuss a person's life or accomplishments until that person has been introduced.*

For example:

> One artist who depicted the lives of the Plains Indians was Karl Bodmer.
> Bodmer was a realist Swiss painter with classical training.

The first sentence introduces Bodmer. The second sentence tells us something about him and what he did. *If a sentence refers to a person by his or her last name only, that person must have been introduced in a previous sentence!*

For example:

> Seventeen-year-old Lady Jane Grey was Queen of England for nine days, in 1553.
> Grey was convicted of treason as a result of a power struggle.

The first sentence introduces Lady Jane Grey. The second sentence refers to her by last name, because now we are already familiar with her.

Details! Details! Details!

Remember: Everything in a paragraph is going to be talking about one main topic, but references to that topic are not always going to be helpful in ordering the sentences! You need to find *specific* details, ones that expand on the main topic, or talk about one aspect of it.

Practice — Reference drill (the answers are on p. 115)

In the following pairs of sentences, say whether the sentence introduces the item in bold type, or makes a reference to it. Mark I for introduce, and R for reference. (Notice that some of the words in bold are paraphrased from one sentence to the next!):

1. ____Excess moisture that accumulates in the clouds falls to the earth as **rain**.

   ____**Rainwater** is absorbed into the earth, and eventually finds its way into bodies of water.

2. ____Even though her friend had begun the process, the experimentation that **Laidlaw** conducted led to startling discoveries.

   ____Until the great physicist Olive **Laidlaw** arrived on the scene, work in her field had been conducted almost entirely by her peer, Khalida Jimenez.

3. ____Still, Ted did not do as well on the **test** as he had hoped.

   ____Despite the fact that he knew the students had a copy, the teacher insisted on giving the same history **test** he had used the previous year.

4. ____A **woman** in a hospital has a series of routine tests done.

   ____The doctor then analyzes the results, and informs the **patient** of her condition.

Now circle all detail and name references in the examples below with matching shapes to indicate to whom or what they refer.

5. If a field of study adhered to the scientific method, would you consider it a science?

   Q. These processes—hypothesis, experimentation, and conclusion— are all presented assiduously with each detail accurately and meticulously described.

   R. For this reason, many people consider parapsychology—the study of phenomena that cannot be identified in terms of the laws of "common" science—not to be a true science.

   S. However, parapsychologists follow all the methods and mandates of the scientific method.

   T. And so, I again ask, would you consider parapsychology a science?

   U. The scientific method is a series of processes that are used in "common" science.

6. The rickshaw is often associated with the Japanese.

    Q. But, interestingly, it was actually based on an earlier French carriage called the "broutte."

    R. This association stems from the fact that the word *rickshaw* is shortened from the Japanese *jin riki sha*, which means "man-powered carriages."

    S. The person who created this mix of two cultures was probably an American missionary, Jonathan Goble.

    T. From this example, we can see how innovative ideas are born from the merging of three cultures.

    U. Goble commissioned a Japanese artisan to use the "broutte" as a model in making a carriage for his wife.

CONCLUSION WORDS AND PHRASES

A conclusion word or phrase is often found at the beginning of the last sentence of the paragraph. It lets you know that the sentence is going to summarize something you've already read or a point that has already been proven.

For example:

> **Thus**, by reading the *Iliad* and the *Odyssey* today, we can learn about the moral and religious values held by the people who lived when the poems were written.
>
> **Therefore**, ancient Greek theatre still has an effect on modern theatrical performance.

In these examples, "thus" and "therefore" let you know that a point has been made and that the sentences are going to summarize these points as a conclusion.

Two important types of conclusion sentences are:

- Sentences that mirror the first sentence

- Sentences that connect the topic of the passage to a greater meaning or broader topic

Here are some common conclusion words or phrases: *So, Finally, Therefore, In conclusion, Thus*

Practice — Conclusion drill (the answers are on p. 115)

Circle the conclusion words or phrases in the following examples.

1. If a field of study adhered to the scientific method, would you consider it a science?

   Q. These processes—hypothesis, experimentation, and conclusion—are all presented assiduously with each detail accurately and meticulously described.

   R. For this reason, many people consider parapsychology—the study of phenomena that cannot be identified in terms of the laws of "common" science—not to be a true science.

   S. However, parapsychologists follow all the methods and mandates of the scientific method.

   T. And so, I again ask, would you consider parapsychology a science?

   U. The scientific method is a series of processes that are used in "common" science.

2. The rickshaw is often associated with the Japanese.

   Q. But, interestingly, it was actually based on an earlier French carriage called the "broutte."

   R. This association stems from the fact that the word *rickshaw* is shortened from the Japanese *jin riki sha*, which means "man-powered carriages."

   S. The person who created this mix of two cultures was probably an American missionary, Jonathan Goble.

   T. From this example, we can see how innovative ideas are born from the merging of three cultures.

   U. Goble commissioned a Japanese artisan to use the "broutte" as a model in making a carriage for his wife.

THE TECHNIQUES

What you've just been doing—pairing up sentences—is the technique you'll use to crack the scrambled paragraphs. We call this The Dating Game, because you've been pairing them up on dates, so to speak. Once you pair up two sentences, go to the answers and eliminate any answer choice that doesn't follow the order you've determined thus far.

Don't rely on your memory for anything. Make sure you underline, circle, and make notes about the orders of the choices as you go along.

Ignore the directions! They tell you to use the lines next to the sentences—**don't**! You'll jot down your own order as you make your decisions.

THE DATING GAME

Take a pair of sentences and make a date.

Use references and introductions to link pairs of sentences.

Beware: References are sometimes *too* general (like "rickshaw" or "Japan"), and may refer to the main topic of the paragraph. When you put sentences in order, you need to find specific references that are expanding upon an idea or thing mentioned in another sentence.

Work one pair at a time, jotting down the order of the sentences and crossing off answer choices that do not agree with your list.

Put sentences together! Look for pronouns or references.

Practice — The dating game (the answers are on p. 116)

Try the following example:

1. Many people believe that Alaska is just an icy, barren land.

_____ **Q.** It is teeming with novel opportunities for the nature lover, from unique wildlife to majestic natural scenery found nowhere else in the United States.

_____ **R.** However, Alaska, the 49th state to be admitted to the United States of America, is a land of many natural wonders.

_____ **S.** Alaska has all this and more, but we will lose it all if we do not protect the environment and learn to respect and care for nature.

_____ **T.** In addition to that living wonder, Alaska is home to the highest mountain in North America and to the largest active volcanic crater in the world.

_____ **U.** For example, only here can one see the Kodiak bear, the largest of all the world's flesh-eating animals, in its natural habitat.

The first sentence is	Ⓠ	Ⓡ	Ⓢ	Ⓣ	Ⓤ
The second sentence is	Ⓠ	Ⓡ	Ⓢ	Ⓣ	Ⓤ
The third sentence is	Ⓠ	Ⓡ	Ⓢ	Ⓣ	Ⓤ
The fourth sentence is	Ⓠ	Ⓡ	Ⓢ	Ⓣ	Ⓤ
The fifth sentence is	Ⓠ	Ⓡ	Ⓢ	Ⓣ	Ⓤ

Now check your answer.

One Final Thought

Think before you bubble. Double check the order you are considering and be certain that the sentences flow smoothly and that the transitions and references are clear.

Lastly, for any paragraph you can't piece together, guess quickly and move on!

Practice — Scrambled paragraph drill (the answers are on p. 116)

1.   The need for a "people moving" system other than the elevated trains ("els"), had been obvious for some time.

____ **Q.**   The "els" were noisy and smoky, and their tracks blocked out sunshine, making the quality of life poor where they were situated.

____ **R.**   Eventually it expanded to connect four of the five boroughs of New York City.

____ **S.**   An underground transportation system would eliminate these problems.

____ **T.**   As it expanded, the subway took over, and in the end the "els" disappeared.

____ **U.**   One such system, the New York City subway, was opened in 1904 by the Interborough Rapid Transit Corporation.

The first sentence is   Ⓠ   Ⓡ   Ⓢ   Ⓣ   Ⓤ
The second sentence is   Ⓠ   Ⓡ   Ⓢ   Ⓣ   Ⓤ
The third sentence is   Ⓠ   Ⓡ   Ⓢ   Ⓣ   Ⓤ
The fourth sentence is   Ⓠ   Ⓡ   Ⓢ   Ⓣ   Ⓤ
The fifth sentence is   Ⓠ   Ⓡ   Ⓢ   Ⓣ   Ⓤ

2.   During the Great Depression of the 1930s, women lost much of the ground they had gained in professional status, work rights, and salary.

____ **Q.**   However, when World War II began, women filled the positions vacated by war-bound men.

____ **R.**   The few paying jobs that remained during this time went mostly to men.

____ **S.**   Their effective work in these positions proved that there is no occupation that is solely masculine or feminine.

____ **T.**   America was still adhering to the notion of the man as breadwinner.

____ **U.**   They flourished in factories, offices, and industry, on farms, and as teachers in colleges.

The first sentence is   Ⓠ   Ⓡ   Ⓢ   Ⓣ   Ⓤ
The second sentence is   Ⓠ   Ⓡ   Ⓢ   Ⓣ   Ⓤ
The third sentence is   Ⓠ   Ⓡ   Ⓢ   Ⓣ   Ⓤ
The fourth sentence is   Ⓠ   Ⓡ   Ⓢ   Ⓣ   Ⓤ
The fifth sentence is   Ⓠ   Ⓡ   Ⓢ   Ⓣ   Ⓤ

3.   The musical has been called the only true "American" theater form.

___ Q.   All other forms of theater were developed elsewhere, most before the United States existed.

___ R.   It flourished from the 1920s to 1950s as the home for popular songwriters.

___ S.   Today, they are even referred to as "Broadway musicals," because that is still the place where they are showcased.

___ T.   The first musicals, however, were written in the early 1900s in New York for theaters on Broadway.

___ U.   For example, drama has been around since the ancient Greeks, opera was developed in Europe during the Renaissance, and even operetta came from Europe in the 1800s.

The first sentence is   Ⓠ   Ⓡ   Ⓢ   Ⓣ   Ⓤ
The second sentence is   Ⓠ   Ⓡ   Ⓢ   Ⓣ   Ⓤ
The third sentence is   Ⓠ   Ⓡ   Ⓢ   Ⓣ   Ⓤ
The fourth sentence is   Ⓠ   Ⓡ   Ⓢ   Ⓣ   Ⓤ
The fifth sentence is   Ⓠ   Ⓡ   Ⓢ   Ⓣ   Ⓤ

4.   Few people have made so strong an impact on New York City that their efforts are still influential today.

___ Q.   New Yorkers now enjoy many places that would not exist but for one of these people: Robert Moses.

___ R.   He could do all of this because during his career he held several appointed positions in New York's government.

___ S.   For instance, the Henry Hudson Parkway, the Triborough Bridge, Lincoln Center, and Jones Beach State Park are all projects Moses guided to completion.

___ T.   He was the head of the Triborough Bridge and Tunnel Authority, as well as Parks Commissioner.

___ U.   He is responsible for many of the highways, bridges, tunnels, and parks that New Yorkers use on a daily basis.

The first sentence is   Ⓠ   Ⓡ   Ⓢ   Ⓣ   Ⓤ
The second sentence is   Ⓠ   Ⓡ   Ⓢ   Ⓣ   Ⓤ
The third sentence is   Ⓠ   Ⓡ   Ⓢ   Ⓣ   Ⓤ
The fourth sentence is   Ⓠ   Ⓡ   Ⓢ   Ⓣ   Ⓤ
The fifth sentence is   Ⓠ   Ⓡ   Ⓢ   Ⓣ   Ⓤ

5. The painter Gerhard Richter said that abstract art is a way to approach "that which cannot be grasped or understood."

____ **Q.** That is, the abstract painter simply attempts to express the inexpressible.

____ **R.** The Modern Abstractionists, however, were interested in new challenges.

____ **S.** For centuries before the advent of this art form, it had been acceptable to paint only the material world.

____ **T.** They explored with shape, color, and gesture, developing a new language.

____ **U.** This "language" transmitted a lasting excitement to modern art.

The first sentence is	Q	R	S	T	U
The second sentence is	Q	R	S	T	U
The third sentence is	Q	R	S	T	U
The fourth sentence is	Q	R	S	T	U
The fifth sentence is	Q	R	S	T	U

6. Some people think that going to the amusement park is just a walk in the park.

____ **Q.** But such an excursion is a serious decision that requires great thought, much preparation, and a clear head.

____ **R.** Someone who eats before a ride on the "Wall of Death" could make the experience unpleasant for the other passengers.

____ **S.** So, as you see, going to the amusement park is no trivial or simple fun-filled event, but rather a harrowing and serious series of important decisions.

____ **T.** The first decision, of many that have to be made, involves whether to eat before or after going on a ride.

____ **U.** Then one needs to consider what type of ride is most suitable: water rides, up and down rides, spinning rides, rolling rides, or rocking rides.

The first sentence is	Q	R	S	T	U
The second sentence is	Q	R	S	T	U
The third sentence is	Q	R	S	T	U
The fourth sentence is	Q	R	S	T	U
The fifth sentence is	Q	R	S	T	U

7. The grid pattern of New York City's streets was created in 1811 by John
    Randall, Jr.

_____ Q. Randall was forced to begin the cross streets of the grid with First Street, immedi-
          ately above Houston, since the area below Houston Street was already settled.

_____ R. The idea of a grid enabled him to plan a map of Manhattan, including areas that
          were uninhabited at that time.

_____ S. On the other hand, the avenues ran the full length of the island, beginning with
          First Avenue near the East River.

_____ T. As New Yorkers know, Broadway runs the length of the island on a diagonal from
          northwest to southeast.

_____ U. The only major exception to these perpendicular streets and avenues is the old
          Bloomingdale Road, known today as Broadway.

The first sentence is	Q	R	S	T	U
The second sentence is	Q	R	S	T	U
The third sentence is	Q	R	S	T	U
The fourth sentence is	Q	R	S	T	U
The fifth sentence is	Q	R	S	T	U

8. Virginia Woolf is best known as a novelist, but her works include many
    essays and short works of fiction.

_____ Q. For example, her famous essay "A Room of One's Own" voiced certain feminist
          principles obscured by plot and character in her fiction.

_____ R. No matter which of the three she wrote, she worked constantly to polish her
          unique writing style.

_____ S. Specifically, Woolf often used short fiction to experiment with new styles and
          techniques which later influenced her novels.

_____ T. This experimentation is also visible in her nonfiction writings, which are not
          technically "short stories."

_____ U. This can be seen in her first short story, "Phyllis and Rosamond," which was
          published before her first novel.

The first sentence is	Q	R	S	T	U
The second sentence is	Q	R	S	T	U
The third sentence is	Q	R	S	T	U
The fourth sentence is	Q	R	S	T	U
The fifth sentence is	Q	R	S	T	U

6

Answer Key to SHSAT Drills

FUNDAMENTALS

MATH VOCABULARY TEST (PAGE 21)

1.	6	0, 1, 2, 3, 4, and 5
2.	2, 4, 6	Many sets of integers would answer this question
3.	3	3, 5, and 7
4.	8	
5.	That number	The smallest positive integer is 1, and any number times 1 is itself.
6.	90	$5 \times 6 \times 3 = 90$
7.	30	$3 + 11 + 16 = 30$
8.	60	$90 - 30 = 60$
9.	2, 4, 6	Your answer to number 2, as long as your integers are positive, answers this one too!
10.	Yes	
11.	22	$5 + 6 + 4 + 7 = 22$
12.	D	The numbers are 4, 5, 6, 7, and 8. 8 squared (8×8) equals 64.

ORDER OF OPERATIONS (PAGE 22)

1. 9
2. 16
3. 7
4. 5
5. 6
6. 30
7. 70
8. 60
9. 20
10. 100

FACTORS (PAGE 23)

1. D
2. J
3. B

MULTIPLES (PAGE 24)

1. B
2. J
3. D
4. H

REDUCING FRACTIONS (PAGE 26)

1. $\dfrac{3}{4}$

2. $\dfrac{1}{5}$

3. $\dfrac{2}{3}$

4. $\dfrac{3}{8}$

5. $\dfrac{3}{4}$

6. $\dfrac{2}{7}$

7. 1

8. $1\dfrac{2}{9}$ or $\dfrac{11}{9}$

9. If the numerator is bigger than the denominator, the fraction is greater than 1.

ADDING AND SUBTRACTING FRACTIONS (PAGE 27)

1. $\dfrac{25}{24}$ or $1\dfrac{1}{24}$

2. $\dfrac{17}{24}$

3. $\dfrac{6}{7}$ Did you use the Bowtie here? There was a common denominator already!

4. $\dfrac{1}{12}$

5. $\dfrac{73}{36}$ or $2\dfrac{1}{36}$

6. $-\dfrac{7}{20}$

5. $\dfrac{13}{3}$ or $4\dfrac{1}{3}$

8. $\dfrac{2}{9}$

9. $\dfrac{49}{60}$

10. $\dfrac{6x}{6} = x$

MULTIPLYING AND DIVIDING FRACTIONS (PAGE 28)

1. $\frac{1}{3}$

2. $\frac{5}{4}$ or $1\frac{1}{4}$

3. $\frac{6}{25}$

4. 1

5. $\frac{4}{5}$

FRACTION PROBLEMS (PAGE 29)

1. B
2. H
3. D
4. F
5. D Did you use the bowtie to add all those fractions? If so, look for an easier way to combine things: $\frac{1}{3} + \frac{1}{4} = 1$ and $\frac{2}{3} + \frac{1}{3} = 1$, etc.

DECIMALS (PAGE 31)

1. 18.7
2. 4.19
3. 4.78
4. 10.625
5. .018
6. 6000
7. 5
8. D
9. H

EXPONENTS (PAGE 32)

1. 8
2. 16
3. 27
4. 64
5. B
6. G

ALGEBRA

MANIPULATE (PAGE 34)

1. 3
2. 5
3. 6
4. 7
5. 4
6. 8
7. 8
8. $\frac{1}{4}$
9. 7
10. 7 Number 9 and number 10 are really the same question. Did you see it?
11. 7
12. D
13. J Be careful! If you chose (F), you did all the work, but didn't answer the right question!
14. B Be careful of answer choice (E)!
15. J

FUNCTIONS (PAGE 35)

1. B
2. H
3. D
4. J
5. A

TRANSLATING AND SOLVING PERCENT QUESTIONS (PAGE 37)

1. 12
2. 24
3. 5
4. 80

WORD PROBLEMS INVOLVING PERCENTAGES (PAGE 37)

1. E
2. H
3. C
4. K
5. A
6. K
7. C
8. H
9. A
10. F

Ratios (Page 39)

1. E
2. H
3. C
4. G
5. C
6. H

Average Problems (Page 41)

1. A   Be careful of (B)—what does the question ask for?
2. J
3. B
4. K
5. E

Plugging In (Page 43)

1. E
2. J
3. E
4. K
5. C   If you had trouble, try plugging in 8 for the number of pieces in the pie, drawing
      a pie with eight pieces, and crossing pieces off as Miguel eats them.
6. G
7. C
8. H

Backsolving (Page 47)

1. C
2. K
3. C
4. G
5. D

GEOMETRY

PERIMETER (PAGE 50)

1. D
2. H
3. C

TRIANGLES (PAGE 53)

1. A
2. H
3. A
4. G

AREA AND VOLUME (PAGE 56)

1. C Backsolve!
2. J
3. B
4. J

CHARTS AND GRAPHS

CHART AND GRAPH PROBLEMS (PAGE 60)

1. E
2. J
3. E Be careful of (A)—look at the little note underneath the chart!
4. J
5. B
6. K
7. B
8. H

MATH REVIEW (PAGE 63)

1. Yes
2. It is neither positive nor negative
3. Addition
4. Multiplication
5. The quotient
6. Yes; No
7. Exponents
8. Yes; No
9. No; Yes
10. Zero
11. Two
12. $2 \times 2 \times 2 = 8$
13. Over 100
14. Multiplication
15. Total
16. Average pie
17. Plug in a number
18. Add; All four
19. Multiply; Two
20. 180
21. 3; 180
22. 360
23. 2; equilateral
24. Hypotenuse; right angle
25. Area (of a triangle) $= \dfrac{1}{2}$ base $\times$ height

READING

GETTING THROUGH THE PASSAGE (PAGE 69)

You should have brief labels like the following:

Label for first paragraph: Norway → Iceland

Label for second paragraph: Iceland → Greenland

Label for third paragraph: lost

Label for fourth paragraph: saw America; landed Greenland

What? a Viking

So What? found America early

Passage type? history of an event

ANSWERING A GENERAL QUESTION (PAGE 71)

1. D
2. H
3. D

ANSWERING A SPECIFIC QUESTION (PAGE 75)

1. C
2. F   Lead word: Iceland
3. B
4. K   Lead word: Greenland

ELIMINATING ANSWERS (PAGE 77)

For a general question

A   Too big—she or he can't do that in a few paragraphs
C   Extreme
D   Extreme
E   Extreme
F   Extreme
H   Too small—this is only a detail

For a tone/attitude question

J
K
M
O   Too extreme, even though it's positive!
P
Q
S
T   Why would anyone write about something she/he doesn't care about?

For a specific question

U   Extreme
V   Extreme
X   Extreme and against common sense

ALL READING TECHNIQUES (PAGE 79)

What? tides
So What? are caused by the Moon

1. A
2. J
3. E
4. H

LOGICAL REASONING

GAMES DRILL (PAGE 88)

1. E
2. F
3. D
4. F
5. E
6. F
7. E
8. K
9. C
10. K
11. D
12. H

SCRAMBLED PARAGRAPHS

TRANSITION DRILL (PAGE 93)

1. In line R, "For this reason" is a transition phrase that indicates that this sentence is continuing in
    the same direction as a previous sentence.
    In line S, "However" is a transition indicating a different direction.
    In line T, "And" and "again" are transition words continuing the direction.
2. In line Q, "But" is a transition word indicating a change of direction.
    In line T, "From this example" is a transition phrase continuing the direction.

Pronoun Drill (Page 94)

1. In the opening statement, "you" refers to the reader, and "it" refers to a field of study.
   In line Q "these" refers to "hypothesis, experimentation and conclusion" directly following.
   In line R, "this reason" refers to the information in line S.
   In line T, "I" refers to "the author" and "you" refers to the reader.
   In line U be careful, the word "that" is **not** used as a pronoun here.
2. In line Q, "it" refers to the rickshaw.
   In line T, "this example" also refers to the rickshaw, and "we" refers to the readers and author.
   In line U, "his" refers to Jonathan Goble.

Reference Drill (Page 96)

1. Introduce
   Reference
2. Reference
   Introduce
3. Reference
   Introduce
4. Introduce
   Reference
5. In line R, "parapsychology" is introduced and matches up with the reference to "parapsychologists,"in S, and "parapsychology" in T, so we can put R before S and before T.
   In line U, "'common' science" is introduced and is referred to in line R, so U comes before R.
   In line U, "processes" is introduced and is referred to in line Q, so U is before Q.
   In line R "for this reason" refers to all of line Q, so U is before Q.
   Now we can jot down a rough order of four sentences:

   >   U   Q   R   S
   >   T

6. In line R, "this association" refers to the opening statement "associated," so R goes first.
   In line S, "Jonathan Goble" is introduced and is referred to in line U.
   Line T refers to "three cultures": Japan is mentioned everywhere, but "French" in Q and "American" in S must come before T.
   In line Q "broutte" is introduced and referred to in line U, so Q is before U.
   Now we can jot down a rough order for these four sentences:

   >   R   S   U   T
   >   Q

   We know that S and Q are before T and U, but we don't know the order between S and Q, so make sure you don't indicate anything that you don't know when you're jotting down your order.

Conclusion Drill (Page 98)

1. Line T starts off with "And so," indicating that it probably comes last.
2. No sentence contains a conclusion word. Although line T seems to be summing things up at the end, it could merely be indicating that it may be towards the end of the paragraph.

The Dating Game (Page 99)

1. Line R introduces "Alaska" and Alaska is referred to as "It" in line Q. Our first date:
   R and Q.
   Line U names the Kodiak bear, mentioned in Q. So Q and U are a date.
   Line T mentions "that living wonder"—what living wonder could that be? The only living thing mentioned is "the Kodiak bear" in Line U, so we have our third date: U and T.
   Line S mentions that "Alaska has all this and more," all what? All that stuff we just read about in T and U, the Kodiak bear, and the volcanic crater. So, U and T come before S.
   R Q U T S

Scrambled Paragraphs (Page 100)

1. QSURT
2. RTQUS
3. QUTRS
4. QUSRT
5. QSRTU
6. QTRUS
7. RQSUT
8. SUTQR

III

Practice Test and Explanations

7
Practice Test

Suggested Time — 75 Minutes

45 Questions

SCRAMBLED PARAGRAPHS

Paragraphs 1–5

DIRECTIONS: In this section, arrange each group of sentences to create the best paragaph. The first sentence for each paragraph is given; the remaining five sentences are listed in random order. Choose the order for these five sentences that will create the **best** paragraph, one that is well-organized, logical, and grammatically correct. Each correctly ordered paragraph is worth double the value of a question in any other section of the test. No credit will be given for responses that are only partially correct.

To keep track of your sentence order, use the blanks to the left of the sentences. For example, write "2" next to the sentence you think follows the first sentence, "3" next to the sentence you think follows "2," and so on. You may change these numbers if you decide on a different order. When you are satisfied with your sentence order, mark your choices on your answer sheet.

PARAGRAPH 1

Insects do not have spoken communications, but they have other forms of communication that are equally effective.

_____ **Q.** Different insects use different methods of communication.

_____ **R.** Ants, on the other hand, leave behind specific scent trails to mark paths to food and danger.

_____ **S.** Ants and bees, for example, are able to share large amounts of complex information without talking in two completely different, silent ways.

_____ **T.** If after these two examples it seems strange that insects can communicate, just imagine how we must seem to them.

_____ **U.** Bees do this by dancing out complex patterns that tell other bees where they can find food or water.

CONTINUE ON TO THE NEXT PAGE →

PARAGRAPH 2

Most people believe that when Christopher Columbus landed in America, in 1492, he was the first European to do so.

_____ Q. Recent archaeological evidence has supported alternate theories.

_____ R. When these remains were examined, the settlement was found to have been occupied in about 1000 A.D.

_____ S. However, as the twentieth century has progressed, that belief has been challenged.

_____ T. For instance, in 1963, scientists uncovered the remains of a Viking settlement on the northern tip of Newfoundland.

_____ U. Therefore, despite popular belief, the Vikings were colonizing the new world long before Christopher Columbus arrived.

PARAGRAPH 3

The American anole, a small desert lizard, is a pretender among pretenders.

_____ Q. For example, when an anole sits on a plant during a warm, dry, summer day its color is a bright, emerald green.

_____ R. Sometimes mistaken for a chameleon, it does not change color to match its surroundings, as real chameleons do.

_____ S. Often thought to be just like other lizards, this desert lizard actually has its own special characteristics.

_____ T. But when it is uncovered among dead leaves in the wintertime it appears a dark brown.

_____ U. Unlike the chameleon, the anole only changes color in response to temperature.

CONTINUE ON TO THE NEXT PAGE ➞

PARAGRAPH 4

When most people think of spiders, they think of the webs that spiders weave.

_____ Q. However, even though the spider webs take a beautiful form, they also serve a deadly function.

_____ R. At first glance, spider webs appear intricate and beautifully crafted.

_____ S. One example is the wolf spider, which wanders its territory in search of prey.

_____ T. However, not all spiders spin these delicate and dangerous webs; some have more direct methods.

_____ U. For most spiders, it is their primary means of trapping the insects that make up their diet.

PARAGRAPH 5

Even though music seems to be a part of every human society, why people respond to it is a mystery.

_____ Q. One answer might be that our aptitude for music is related to our aptitude for language, but music is not just language in another form.

_____ R. When one composer suffered difficulty in communicating after he had a stroke on the left side of the brain (the side associated with language) he was still able to write beautiful compositions.

_____ S. On the other hand, when another composer experienced damage to the right side of his brain, he was still able to speak well, but lost much of his interest in music.

_____ T. This would seem to hint that there is actually an area in our brains that is responsible for our musicality.

_____ U. Why do most people throughout the world, people of every religion and culture, play and enjoy music?

CONTINUE ON TO THE NEXT PAGE ➞

LOGICAL REASONING

QUESTIONS 11–12

DIRECTIONS: Read the information given and choose the **best** answer to each question. Base your answer **only on the information given.**

In a logical reasoning test, certain words must be read with caution. For example, "The red house is **between** the yellow and the blue houses," does not necessarily mean "The red house is **between and next to** the yellow and blue houses"; one or more other houses may separate the red house from the yellow house or from the blue house. This precaution also applies to words such as **above**, **below**, **before**, **after**, **ahead of**, and **behind**.

11. Four friends go skydiving. Jane jumps after Fred. Tim jumps first. Mary jumps before Jane, but after Fred.

    In what order did they leave the plane?

    A. Tim, Fred, Mary, Jane
    B. Tim, Fred, Jane, Mary
    C. Fred, Mary, Jane, Tim
    D. Mary, Jane, Tim, Fred
    E. Cannot be determined from the information given.

12. Last Saturday, Mark spent most of the day watching television. He watched three cartoons, two football games, and one movie. After watching television, he ate dinner with his family.

    According to the information given, which statement **must** be true?

    F. Mark's family watched television with him.
    G. Mark enjoyed the cartoons more than the football games.
    H. The movie was longer than any of the other programs Mark watched.
    J. Mark watched a greater number of cartoons than football games.
    K. Mark started watching television before ten in the morning.

CONTINUE ON TO THE NEXT PAGE ⟶

13. A dog hears higher sounds than a human does. A cat can see better in dim light than a human normally can. A shark can pick up electric signals that humans cannot sense.

Based on the information above, which of the following is a valid conclusion?

A. All animals have sensory abilities superior to humans' sensory abilities.
B. Some animals have sensory abilities that are different from humans' sensory abilities.
C. Dogs have better hearing than cats.
D. Scientists should not be surprised to find that all of a cat's senses are stronger than a dog's senses.
E. Humans do not have sensory abilities that are superior to any animal's sensory abilities.

14. At a picnic there are three boys, Maurice, Bill, and Charles, and three girls, Kysha, Leigh and Francesca. There are three pairs of brothers and sisters. Maurice is not related to Francesca. Bill is Kysha's brother.

Of the following, which is the correct pairing of brothers and sisters?
F. Maurice and Kysha, Bill and Leigh, Charles and Francesca
G. Maurice and Francesca, Bill and Kysha, Charles and Leigh
H. Maurice and Leigh, Bill and Francesca, Charles and Kysha
J. Maurice and Leigh, Bill and Kysha, Charles and Francesca
K. Maurice and Kysha, Bill and Francesca, Charles and Leigh

15. In the code below, each letter stands for one of two words in a pair. The letters are not necessarily in the same order as the words. Each letter always represents the same word.

L G means "beach ball"
C L means "ball point"
C R means "point blank"
N R means "blank slate"
N P means "slate blue"
P S means "blue beard"

How would you write "blue beach" in this code?

A. P G
B. S L
C. L P
D. C S
E. N S

16. Brenda notices that the neighbor's dog, Sparky, is barking. She concludes that it must now be 7 P.M.

Without any other information, which of the following statements must be true in order for Brenda's conclusion to be valid?

F. Sparky usually barks at 7 P.M.
G. There has been no barking for several days.
H. The only time Sparky barks is at 7 P.M.
J. The other dogs in the neighborhood are not barking.
K. It has been almost twenty-four hours since Brenda has last heard Sparky bark.

CONTINUE ON TO THE NEXT PAGE →

Questions 17 and 18 refer to the following information.

Two girls, Andrea and Danielle, and three boys, Bob, Christopher, and Edward, are at the movies. They are sitting in a single row of five seats numbered 1 through 5.

1) Andrea is not sitting next to Bob.
2) Christopher is in seat number 2.
3) Bob is not sitting next to a boy.
4) Christopher is sitting next to Andrea.

17. Who is in seat number 5?

A. Andrea
B. Bob
C. Edward
D. Danielle
E. Cannot be determined from the information given.

18. Who is in seat number 1?

F. Danielle
G. Christopher
H. Edward
J. Andrea
K. Cannot be determined from the information given.

---

19. If a = 2, b = 3, c = 4, . . . , z = 27, what combination of letters would spell "Batman"?

A. 2, 3, 14, 15, 19, 2
B. 1, 2, 13, 1, 1, 18
C. 3, 2, 21, 14, 2, 15
D. 3, 2, 19, 2, 14, 15
E. 2, 1, 18, 1, 13, 14

20. All violinists who practice often and play many concerts will become world-famous. Victoria practices her violin often. Therefore, Victoria will become world-famous.

Which of the following uses reasoning that is most like the reasoning used in the paragraph above?

F. All bananas that are put in the refrigerator will turn black. This banana has been placed in the refrigerator. Therefore, this banana will turn black.
G. All sports are fun. Baseball is a sport. Therefore, baseball is fun.
H. All cakes that use the proper ingredients and are baked properly will taste delicious. This cake includes the proper ingredients. Therefore, this cake will be delicious.
J. All schools have classrooms and desks. This building has classrooms and desks. Therefore, this building is a school.
K. All fish live in water. Sharks are a type of fish. Therefore, sharks live in water.

CONTINUE ON TO THE NEXT PAGE →

READING

QUESTIONS 21–50

DIRECTIONS: Read each passage below and answer the questions following it. Base your answers **only on information contained in the passage**. You may reread a passage if you need to. Mark the **best** answer for each question.

Many contemporary scientists believe the universe began in a giant explosion, or "big bang." At least ten billion years ago, they surmise, extremely
5 high temperatures and pressure caused the universe to expand rapidly from a compressed state. Soon after, significant cooling occurred, and at this point there were probably many types of el-
10 ementary particles present. As further cooling occurred, certain nuclei were formed. Gradually, over millions of years, the universe began to take on the characteristics that we observe today.

15 One of the major assumptions upon which the big bang theory is dependent is called the cosmological principle. This principle states that our observations of general properties of the
20 universe do not depend on our location or the direction in which we look. Based on this assumption, scientists believe that the explosion known as the big bang occurred not at any particular
25 point, but instantaneously throughout space.

Evidence to support the big bang theory comes mainly from observations of galaxies beyond the Milky Way.
30 These galaxies are so far away that, by the time light from them reaches us, millions of years have passed. Distant objects are seen as they appeared when the light we receive first left them,
35 providing us with a picture of the early universe.

In addition, the discovery of weak radiation in space has given support to the big bang theory of the origin of the uni-
40 verse. This low-level static, observed to come from every direction, is believed to be the remains of the initial fireball. At the very beginning, the fireball was unimaginably hot. This heat accounts
45 for the radiation we now detect.

21. Which of the following best tells what the passage is about?

A. a proof of the origin of the universe
B. an explanation of how scientists derived the age of the universe
C. a consideration of one major use of static
D. a proof of the existence of galaxies other than our own
E. a discussion of evidence for one theory of the origin of the universe

CONTINUE ON TO THE NEXT PAGE →

22. In order to support the big bang theory, the author mentions which of the following?

    F. the results of Galileo's research
    G. the discovery of low-level radiation
    H. the presence of lead in the initial fireball
    J. the exact temperature of the initial fireball
    K. the names of scientists who performed the studies

23. The discussion in lines 3–12 of the change in temperature implies that

    A. gradually, the Earth moved into a period known today as an ice age.
    B. nuclei have always been present.
    C. elementary particles are never found under extreme temperatures.
    D. nuclei did not exist under the extreme heat of the initial explosion.
    E. scientists will never know at what point nuclei began to be formed.

24. The discussion of the cosmological principle suggests that

    F. scientists sometimes have to base their theories on other theories.
    G. scientists will never be able to concretely prove the big bang theory.
    H. we cannot make direct observations of the characteristics of the universe.
    J. the big bang started in Detroit, Michigan.
    K. scientists cannot base their theories on fact.

25. In what way is measurement of the speed of light useful for scientists researching the big bang theory?

    A. Scientists can measure the speed and force of the explosion.
    B. The light distorts the images the scientists are observing.
    C. Knowing the speed of light in part provides scientists with knowledge about the universe as it once was.
    D. Scientists are able to observe the explosion as it happened.
    E. The light from the explosion has allowed scientists to make other observations in the night sky.

26. According to the final paragraph, what is one characteristic of the static that caused scientists to associate it with the big bang?

    F. The radiation was created as the universe cooled.
    G. The low-level static does not seem to be coming from one specific place.
    H. The initial fireball was comprised mostly of static.
    J. The initial explosion was equivalent in magnitude to a nuclear explosion.
    K. The low-level static was caused by a constant source of heat, over a long period of time.

CONTINUE ON TO THE NEXT PAGE →

Kangaroos are fascinating creatures because they are so different from other mammals. Unlike most mammals, kangaroos rear their young in a
5 pouch and hop to get around. Their long, powerful hind legs are used for jumping, and their thick tail gives them balance. Their forelimbs are used almost like human hands. Despite these
10 well-known characteristics, prevalent among all kangaroos, there are many lesser-known variations; some kangaroo species vary tremendously in such distinguishing characteristics as habitat,
15 color, social patterns, and size. (They range in length from nine inches to more than eight feet.)

The explanation often given for these odd features is that kangaroos are mar-
20 supials, and marsupials are a primitive form of mammal. This explanation, which may or may not be correct, is particularly popular among people who live in the Northern Hemisphere.
25 Their view is reflected in the statements they make about the Virginia opossum, the only marsupial native to North America. The opossum is frequently described as a primitive animal, little
30 changed since the time of dinosaurs. There is some evidence for such statements. For example, fossils of marsupials that existed at the same time as dinosaurs, some 100 million years ago,
35 have been classified as belonging to the same group as the Virginia opossum.

But even if the opossum can in some ways be considered a "living fossil," the same cannot be said about the kanga-
40 roo. These Australian marsupials of the Macropodidae (literally, "big feet") family have changed recently in order to adapt to a changing environment.

This is a very common occurrence in
45 the evolutionary patterns of all animals. In fact, almost every family of animals, from fish to insects to mammals, have changed form in some way since their ancient ancestors roamed the earth.
50 Even plants and trees, seemingly the same as they were eons ago, exhibit characteristics that are relatively new to them. In the case of the Macropodidae, they evolved from small forest animals
55 into ones that live mainly in open spaces. This development was probably related to the spread of grassland areas in Australia between ten and fifteen million years ago.

27. Which of the following best tells what this passage is about?

   A. a comparison of the opossum and the kangaroo
   B. the competition between marsupials and dinosaurs
   C. the evolutionary background of kangaroos
   D. how kangaroos are not really mammals
   E. the importance of fossils in research

28. The author of the passage most likely agrees with which of the following statements?

   F. Opossums are smarter than kangaroos.
   G. Dinosaurs ate kangaroo meat.
   H. Kangaroos were once extinct.
   J. Kangaroos are not real mammals.
   K. Kangaroos are interesting animals.

CONTINUE ON TO THE NEXT PAGE →

29. The author of the passage is most likely

    A. a hunter.
    B. a business man.
    C. a cowboy.
    D. an Australian.
    E. a scientist.

30. The author most likely quotes the exact size ranges in lines 15–17 in order to

    F. shock the reader.
    G. demonstrate one way in which different species of kangaroos vary greatly.
    H. contradict earlier research.
    J. prove that not all kangaroos are important.
    K. provide evidence that kangaroos have evolved in a variety of ways.

31. The phrase "living fossil" in line 38 refers to which of the following?

    A. a dinosaur
    B. a kangaroo
    C. an opossum
    D. an Australian marsupial
    E. a fossil of a marsupial

32. What does the passage imply about the kangaroo's development?

    F. The kangaroo has adapted to its surroundings more than some other marsupials.
    G. The kangaroo had a development almost identical to that of the opossum.
    H. The kangaroo is similar to a dinosaur.
    J. The kangaroos' native habitat is North America.
    K. Kangaroos look exactly as they looked one million years ago.

CONTINUE ON TO THE NEXT PAGE ➞

Crete was settled about 5000 B.C. by travelers from Greece who journeyed across sixty miles of open water to reach this island in the Mediterranean Sea. Because of the jagged spine of mountains cutting across the land, the settlers realized that the potential for farming was very limited. As a means of survival, the people of Crete focused their attention on their geographical assets: the waters surrounding the island, their strategic position in the Mediterranean, and the natural harbors of the gently sloping northern coasts. Thus, the Cretans were the first people to develop a modern commercial economy based mainly on seafaring and trade.

Using evidence from several sources, we can understand some of the details of Cretan life. Archaeological findings support the legend that the people of Crete were skillful builders. The island's forests provided timber for building ships. Their ships were sea-worthy and must have required careful design and expert construction. Their ships had high, sharply curved bows and sterns, and keels covered in bronze that stood out beyond the prow, a design that shows the boats were intended for ramming into enemy ships. This naval tactic, developed in Crete, dominated sea warfare during this time.

The trading success of the Cretans gave people leisure time for their own enjoyment; bullfights are one example of a popular pastime. Art from that time shows people dressed in colorful clothes, large decorated hats, and fancy jewelry. As the culture developed, Crete became known for its sculpture, pottery, and fresco painting. The remains of villages suggest that the society was middle-class. The palace of the priest-King Minos, was as much a commercial center as it was a palace, demonstrating the importance of trade in the Cretan culture. Because it is relatively poor in resources, however, Crete's history of reliance upon trade has continued, even to the modern day.

33. Which of the following best tells what this passage is about?

    A. a description of an early culture
    B. a demonstration of how ships are built
    C. a proof of the origin of the settlers of Crete
    D. a study of the advantages of a trade-oriented economy
    E. an examination of the relationship between geography and culture

34. According to the passage, all of the following statements about Crete are true **except**:

    F. The land was not suitable for the development of an agricultural economy.
    G. The location of the island helped settlers to make a good living by trade.
    H. The island is surrounded by a border of jagged cliffs.
    J. The island provided a large supply of timber.
    K. People enjoyed watching bullfights.

CONTINUE ON TO THE NEXT PAGE →

35. According to the passage, the people of Crete were known as skilled builders because

   A. they dressed well.
   B. they designed a keel that was very advantageous in sea warfare.
   C. the population had no leisure time.
   D. the palace of Minos was a big building.
   E. the histories of other civilizations document the skills of the Cretans.

36. According to the passage, which of the following describes the most important characteristic of the civilization of Crete?

   F. It was the first to develop bullfighting as a sport.
   G. It was a middle-class society.
   H. It was the first to start an economy based on trade and seafaring.
   J. It was preoccupied with war.
   K. It was unable to develop farming skills.

37. According to the passage, the function of "keels covered in bronze" was

   A. to show religious devotions.
   B. to replace wood in building ships.
   C. to improve the land for farming.
   D. to support local merchants.
   E. to ram enemy ships.

38. The final sentence of the passage suggests that

   F. modern Cretans' reliance on trade is due as much to necessity as to ingenuity.
   G. modern Cretans do not rely on trade to the extent that ancient Cretans did.
   H. modern Cretans rely on trade only to sell manufactured goods.
   J. modern Cretans deeply respect the tradition and history of maritime trade.
   K. modern Cretans' trading patterns are unreliable.

CONTINUE ON TO THE NEXT PAGE ⟶

John Philip Sousa was no Beethoven. Nevertheless, he made a contribution to music. When you say "a Sousa march," almost everyone will know what you are talking about. All of his marches bear the stamp of a vigorous, clear-cut, original musical personality. Above all they are intensely practical. Sousa began studying traditional music theory when he was six. As a teenager, it looked as if he would follow in the footsteps of his father, a trombonist. In 1880, as a member of the U.S. Marine Corps, he became the bandmaster of the Marine Band, where he gradually became known as a bandmaster of incredible precision. The marches he wrote, first for the Marine Band and later for his own band, were intended to set the pace for marching men.

Sousa marches are simple. Their tunes are so uncomplicated, catchy, so melodic, that you can easily underrate them. Simple as they may be, they are unmistakably Sousa's. It took inspiration to write them, even if it was only a small amount of inspiration.

Sousa does stir one important thing: national pride. Today, John Philip Sousa's marches can be heard at a variety of patriotic events. At Memorial Day parades or spectacular Fourth of July fireworks displays, the tunes of Sousa are the overwhelming sentimental favorites of marching bands. When his marches are played, even the most unpatriotic of people suddenly rise to the occasion, sometimes marching along with the beat and whistling the simple yet moving melodies. If one's music were the measure of one's pride in a nation, then John Philip Sousa can be recognized as being intensely proud of America. Likewise, if listening to music can inspire patriotism, then when we listen to Sousa's marches we almost automatically become enveloped with a patriotism unheard of, except maybe in times of national emergencies.

39. Which of the following best tells what this passage is about?

   A. It sets forth a new definition of artistic greatness.
   B. It explains the value of the music of John Philip Sousa.
   C. It emphasizes the importance of band music.
   D. It proves that Sousa was one of the greatest musicians of all time.
   E. It shows that Sousa was more talented than Beethoven.

40. The author would be most likely to use which of the following terms in describing the music of John Philip Sousa?

   F. memorable
   G. peaceful
   H. jazzy
   J. stupid
   K. horrible

41. Sousa's work is "practical" (line 8) in the sense that it is

   A. often imitated by classical musicians.
   B. easy to forget.
   C. easily learned by children.
   D. actually used for military marching.
   E. never actually played.

CONTINUE ON TO THE NEXT PAGE ➞

42. The discussion of the simplicity of Sousa's marches in lines 21–27 suggests that

    F. Sousa's marches are childish.

    G. the simplicity of Sousa's marches is unnecessary.

    H. simple music is superior to complex music.

    J. Sousa did not put much thought into his work.

    K. the simplicity of Sousa's marches does not make them any less admirable.

43. What does the passage imply about the quality of Sousa's work?

    A. It is inferior to composers such as Beethoven and Wagner.

    B. Despite their simplicity, his marches merit consideration as true national classics.

    C. It is a highly complex combination of rhythm, melody, and beat.

    D. The works are good to listen to, but have little practical application.

    E. The works are hardly ever heard in today's musical world.

44. Which of the following is **not** mentioned as an aspect of Sousa's compositions?

    F. Marching bands use them very frequently.

    G. They are not equal to the complex works of Beethoven.

    H. The music is original and clearly the work of Sousa.

    J. Wagner's marches were an early influence on Sousa's works.

    K. Sousa's marches are simple.

CONTINUE ON TO THE NEXT PAGE ⟶

On the surface, Africa changed as radically in the early 1990s as it did in the late 1950s, when colonialism began to give way to self-rule. At that time, regions that were colonies of European nations such as Great Britain, France, Portugal, and Spain gained their independence. Many of these new countries did not, however, truly become free; instead, they fell under the oppressive arm of native dictators. Part of the new upheaval of the 1990s, which was ignited by a worldwide movement supporting civil liberties, has decreased the incidence of human rights' abuses. The movement has also begun to erode the power of dictators who, for three decades, have been running Africa into the ground. No African leader has been immune to the pressure from multi-party elections, a free press, and independent courts. For the most part, Big Men—unelected leaders who operate above the law and refuse to participate in free elections—are still in control, though their power-base is eroding.

The human cost of these political changes has been high. Liberia and Somalia are engaged in political revolutions that are disintegrating into bloodbaths. These oppressive, authoritarian governments have been supplanted by anarchy. As the death toll mounts, it seems that the revolutions will bring only escalated looting and bloodshed instead of the hoped-for free elections and greater civil liberties. In other nations, politically opposed groups have fallen into civil war, and virtually unrestrained violence. Many African countries are experiencing waves of "ethnic cleansing," a term used to describe vast efforts on the part of a particular ethnic group to wipe out any potential opposition.

Paradoxically, amid the fast-changing political movements, most Africans are carrying on with their cultural and social traditions. Their daily existence continues to be shaped by the demands of the extended family and the tribe. Though the political upheavals of recent years contain the seeds of a future that may hold greater freedom and prosperity, the changes to date have only served to heighten most Africans' reliance on their kin, their tribesmen, and themselves.

45. Which of the following best tells what this passage is about?

  A. African leaders operated above the law in the past.
  B. Oppressive African governments of the late 1950s are giving way to communism.
  C. Present-day African revolutions will definitely yield to democracy and great economic wealth.
  D. Africans are experiencing a new reliance on their kin, their tribesmen, and themselves due to the changing political climate in recent years.
  E. The recent political changes in Africa have improved the potential for greater civil liberties but have also resulted in factional violence.

46. The author's attitude toward the "dictators" in lines 16–19 is one of

  F. indifference and apathy.
  G. wholehearted approval.
  H. unbiased speculation.
  J. respect and admiration.
  K. contempt and dislike.

CONTINUE ON TO THE NEXT PAGE ➞

47. The author mentions Liberia and Somalia as examples of

    A. revolutions that progressed to violence.

    B. oppressive governments that have advocated revolutions.

    C. political upheavals that have promoted Africans' self-reliance.

    D. Africans' ability to carry on daily life despite violence and revolution.

    E. governments that advocate a multi-party system.

48. The author would most likely agree with all of the following statements **except**:

    F. Africans rely on their family and their tribes.

    G. Revolutions in Africa have resulted in increased civil liberties and increased violence.

    H. African revolutions are the only effective way to promote change.

    J. Revolutions in Liberia and Somalia have become particularly brutal.

    K. Despite the violence of rebel activities in Africa, the outlook for the future is better now than before any change had occurred.

49. The word "paradoxically" in line 46 is used to describe

    A. the customs and habits of the tribes-men.

    B. the power of the Big Men.

    C. the balance between good and evil.

    D. the contradiction between the impact of political changes and the continuance of daily life.

    E. the impact of political upheavals in the last two years.

50. According to the passage, most Africans

    F. are upset about the political upheavals.

    G. continue living their lives in the same way as before the political upheavals.

    H. think the future will be prosperous.

    J. are independent of their kin.

    K. are fighting in political revolutions.

CONTINUE ON TO THE NEXT PAGE →

PART 2—MATHEMATICS

Suggested Time—75 Minutes

50 QUESTIONS

GENERAL INSTRUCTIONS

Solve each problem. Select the **best** answer from the choices given. Mark the letter of your answer on the answer sheet. You can do your figuring in the test booklet or on paper provided by the proctor. **DO NOT MAKE ANY MARKS ON YOUR ANSWER SHEET OTHER THAN FILLING IN YOUR ANSWER CHOICES.**

IMPORTANT NOTES:

(1) Formulas and definitions of mathematical terms and symbols are **not** provided.

(2) Diagrams other than graphs are **not** necessarily drawn to scale. Do not assume any relationship in a diagram unless it is specifically stated or can be figured out from the information given.

(3) Assume that a diagram is in one plane unless the problem specifically states that it is not.

(4) Graphs are drawn to scale. Unless stated otherwise, you can assume relationships according to appearance. For example, (on a graph) lines that appear to be parallel can be assumed to be parallel; likewise for concurrent lines, straight lines, collinear points, right angles, etc.

(5) Reduce all fractions to the lowest terms.

---

51. $\dfrac{5^2 + 5}{5}$

    A. 5
    B. 6
    C. 10
    D. 25
    E. 26

52. Express 27.8913×100 in scientific notation.

    F. 0.278913×10^3
    G. 0.278913×10^4
    H. 2.78913×10^2
    J. 2.78913×10^3
    K. 27.8913×10^2

CONTINUE ON TO THE NEXT PAGE →

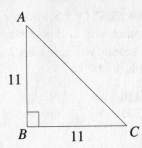

53. The above figure is an isosceles right triangle. The measure of angle C =

A. 90
B. 60
C. 50
D. 45
E. 25

54. A candy bar is advertised as costing "three for $1.00." If Jackie bought 21 candy bars at this price, how much money would she have saved if the price had been reduced to "seven for $2.00"?

F. $1.00
G. $1.50
H. $2.10
J. $3.00
K. $7.00

55. A telephone call costs $1.50 for the first three minutes, and 20 cents for each additional minute. What is the cost of a nine-minute call?

A. $1.70
B. $2.20
C. $2.70
D. $3.30
E. $4.50

56. If $q + r + s = 117$, and $q = s = 4r$, then r =

F. 13
G. 18
H. 30
J. 42
K. 54

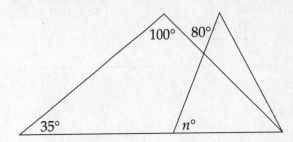

57. In the figure above, what is the value of n?

A. 25
B. 35
C. 45
D. 55
E. 80

58. If the sum of two numbers is 29 and their difference is 7, what is the larger of the two numbers?

F. −18
G. −11
H. 11
J. 12
K. 18

CONTINUE ON TO THE NEXT PAGE ➞

59. Over a five-week period, Tanya sold a total of 90 subscriptions. If she sold 22, 15, 20, and 18 subscriptions in the first four weeks respectively, what was the median number of magazines she sold?

A. 15
B. 18
C. 20
D. 22
E. 25

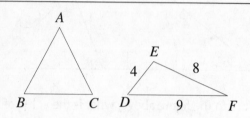

60. For the above figures, the perimeter of triangle ABC equals the perimeter of triangle DEF. If triangle ABC is equilateral, what is the length of side AB?

F. 21
G. 14
H. 10
J. 8
K. 7

61. If $x = -2$ and $y = 4$ then $x^2y + \dfrac{y}{x} =$

A. −18
B. −14
C. 12
D. 14
E. 18

62. Eric has $3.50. Of this amount, he owes his mother 14%, and his sister 76%. How much money will Eric have left after he pays his debts?

F. $0.10
G. $0.35
H. $0.70
J. $0.72
K. $0.84

63. What is the sum of all the distinct prime factors of 48?

A. 5
B. 6
C. 11
D. 36
E. 75

64. Let # be defined by the equation $a \# b = ab + a + b$ for all numbers a and b.

$2 \# 5 =$

F. 7
G. 10
H. 17
J. 20
K. 32

65. If $n \geq 1$, then
$1^n + 1^{n+1} + 1^{n+2} + 1^{n+3} + 1^{n+4} + 1^{n+5} =$

A. 72
B. 15
C. 6
D. 5
E. Cannot be determined from the information given.

CONTINUE ON TO THE NEXT PAGE ⟶

66. What is the decimal representation of $1{,}000 + 1 + \dfrac{1}{1000}$?

    F. 1,001.01
    G. 1,001.001
    H. 1,000.101
    J. 1,000.1001
    K. 1,001.0001

67. A car dealer sells b blue cars and r red cars in one day. Which of the following equations represents the statement, "The number of blue cars sold is three times the number of red cars sold"?

    A. $3r = b$
    B. $3b = r$
    C. $b + 3 = r$
    D. $b = r + 3$
    E. $3b = 3r$

68. $\dfrac{(0.25 + 0.25 + 0.25 + 0.25)}{4} =$

    F. 1.00
    G. 0.75
    H. 0.50
    J. 0.25
    K. 0.125

69. If $5q = 3r = 30$, then $qr =$

    A. 18
    B. 32
    C. 40
    D. 50
    E. 60

70. The following are coordinates of points in the xy-plane. Which of these points is nearest the origin?

    F. $(-1, -1)$
    G. $\left(\dfrac{1}{2}, \dfrac{1}{2}\right)$
    H. $\left(\dfrac{1}{2}, -\dfrac{1}{2}\right)$
    J. $(0, -1)$
    K. $\left(0, \dfrac{1}{2}\right)$

71. If 100 grams is half the mass of one object and twice the mass of another, the mass of the heavier object is how many grams more than the mass of the lighter object?

    A. 200
    B. 150
    C. 100
    D. 75
    E. 50

72. $\dfrac{2}{4} \times \dfrac{3}{6} \times \dfrac{4}{8} \times \dfrac{5}{10} =$

    F. 1
    G. $\dfrac{1}{2}$
    H. $\dfrac{1}{4}$
    J. $\dfrac{1}{8}$
    K. $\dfrac{1}{16}$

CONTINUE ON TO THE NEXT PAGE →

TEMPERATURE IN CITY X ON DEC. 6	
6 a.m.	10° below zero
8 a.m.	2° below zero
10 a.m.	15° above zero

73. What is the average (arithmetic mean) of the temperatures shown on the table above?

    A. 5° above zero
    B. 3° above zero
    C. 1° above zero
    D. 1° below zero
    E. 2° above zero

74. Line segment RT measures 12. Segment ST is $\frac{1}{6}$ of RT. What is the ratio of segment ST to segment RS?

    F. $\frac{1}{6}$

    G. $\frac{1}{5}$

    H. $\frac{1}{3}$

    J. $\frac{5}{6}$

    K. 5

75. If set Q contains all even integers from 4 to 36 inclusive, and set Z contains all multiples of 3, how many integers are common to both sets?

    A. 3
    B. 4
    C. 5
    D. 6
    E. 7

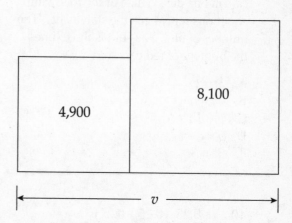

76. The above figure is composed of two squares with areas as shown. What is the value of v?

    F. 70
    G. 90
    H. 140
    J. 160
    K. 180

CONTINUE ON TO THE NEXT PAGE ➔

77. At 4 P.M., a 6-foot-tall man cast a shadow 10 feet long. At the same hour, how long would the shadow of a 15-foot-tall lamp post have been?

A. 9
B. 21
C. 25
D. 27
E. 30

78. What integer satisfies the following equations, $x^2 \leq x$ and $x \leq 0$?

F. 1
G. 0
H. –1
J. An infinite amount.
K. Cannot be determined from the information given.

79. The ratio of apples to bananas at a fruit stand is 5 to 4. The ratio of cherries to bananas is 2 to 5. What is the ratio of apples to cherries?

A. 5:5
B. 5:2
C. 4:5
D. 25:8
E. Cannot be determined from the information given.

80. On Tuesday, $\frac{2}{3}$ of a large block of ice melted. On Wednesday, $\frac{1}{2}$ of the remaining ice melted. If the block of ice then weighed 60 pounds, how much did it weigh, in pounds, at the beginning of the day on Tuesday?

F. 540
G. 480
H. 450
J. 360
K. 180

81. What is the **least** integer greater than –3.7?

A. –4
B. –3
C. 0
D. 1
E. 4

82. If 20% of the science students at Central High study only physics, 25% study only chemistry and the rest study only biology, what is *the smallest number* of science students who could be studying biology?

F. 4
G. 9
H. 11
J. 15
K. 20

CONTINUE ON TO THE NEXT PAGE →

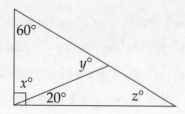

83. In the above triangle, what is the value of z, in terms of x?

    A. $100 - x$

    B. $80 - x$

    C. $x - 40$

    D. $x + 20$

    E. $\dfrac{x}{2}$

84. If $x + 2y = 6$, and $z = 7$, what is the value of $2x + 4y + z$?

    F. 6
    G. 12
    H. 15
    J. 19
    K. 25

85. $(2a^3b^2t^5)^3 =$

    A. $2a^6b^8t^8$
    B. $6a^6b^5t^8$
    C. $6a^6b^4t^{10}$
    D. $8a^9b^6t^{15}$
    E. $8a^{27}b^8t^{125}$

86. A jogger completes one lap around a circular lake with radius $= r$. Another jogger completes one lap around a lake with a radius $= r + 4$. How much further does the second jogger run?

    F. 8
    G. 8π
    H. $8\pi + r$
    J. 16
    K. 16π

87. $\left(\dfrac{1}{2} + \dfrac{2}{5} \right) = \dfrac{9}{10}$

    A. $5\dfrac{2}{3}$

    B. 5.31

    C. 5.00

    D. $4\dfrac{2}{3}$

    E. 4.31

CONTINUE ON TO THE NEXT PAGE ➡

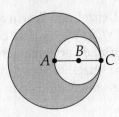

88. A circle with center B is inscribed in a circle with center A such that AC is both the diameter and the radius, respectively, of the two circles. If $BC = 3$, what is the area of the shaded region?

F. 27π
G. 21π
H. 18π
J. 9π
K. 3π

89. If $\dfrac{a}{b} < \dfrac{b}{a}$, $a^2 = 2a$ and $ab = 18$, what is the value of b?

A. 2
B. 3
C. 6
D. 9
E. 18

90. A compact disc is placed in a player that randomly selects and plays songs from the disc. The compact disc contains 3 ballads, 4 instrumental pieces, X dance tracks, and no other pieces. If the probability that the first song played will be a ballad is $\dfrac{1}{4}$, what is the value of X?

F. 1
G. 4
H. 5
J. 9
K. 12

91. What is $-12 - (-10\frac{1}{2})$?

A. $-3\frac{1}{2}$

B. -3

C. $-2\frac{1}{2}$

D. $-1\frac{1}{2}$

E. $1\frac{1}{2}$

92. Kai rides his bicycle up the hill to school and back every day. If he travels twice as fast downhill as up, and it takes 30 minutes round-trip, how far away is his school?

F. 20 miles
G. 18 miles
H. 10 miles
J. 6 miles
K. Cannot be determined from the information given.

CONTINUE ON TO THE NEXT PAGE ⟶

93. An eight-sided die with faces numbered 1 through 8 is rolled twice. What is the probability that the first roll will be 3 and the second roll will be 8 if the die can never be rolled as a 6?

A. $\dfrac{1}{8}$

B. $\dfrac{2}{8}$

C. $\dfrac{2}{7}$

D. $\dfrac{1}{49}$

E. $\dfrac{2}{49}$

94. If , $\dfrac{3n-6}{7-4}=11$ then $n =$

F. 7
G. 9
H. 11
J. 13
K. 15

95. The weight of a barrel when empty is $\dfrac{1}{4}$ of the weight of the water it contains when full. If, when full, the barrel and water weigh a total of 20 pounds, what is the weight, in pounds, of the empty barrel?

A. 4
B. 5
C. 15
D. 16
E. 80

96. Wesley, Denzel, and Earvin all pitched in to buy a VCR. Wesley paid twice as much as Earvin, and Earvin paid three times as much as Denzel. Together, the trio spent $350. How much did Earvin pay?

F. $ 95
G. $105
H. $110
J. $120
K. $160

97. If $x + y = 7$ and $x^2 + y^2 = 25$, what does $2xy$ equal?

A. 14
B. 24
C. 28
D. 36
E. 48

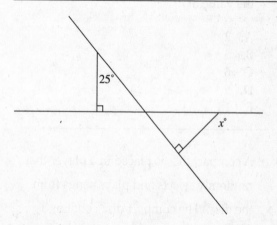

98. In the figure above, $x =$

F. 25
G. 65
H. 155
J. 160
K. 165

CONTINUE ON TO THE NEXT PAGE →

99. $\left(3 \times \dfrac{1}{100}\right) + \left(4 \times \dfrac{1}{10}\right) + \left(5 \times \dfrac{1}{1000}\right) + 6(1)$

    A. 0.6435
    B. 3.456
    C. 6.435
    D. 6.543
    E. 64.35

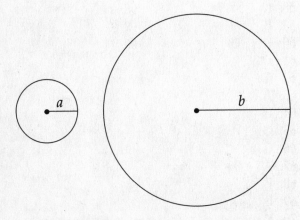

Note: Figure not drawn to scale.

100. In the figure above, two circles have radii of a and b, respectively. If $a = \dfrac{1}{3}b$, and the sum of the circumferences of the two circles is 64, then what is the value of b?

    F. 8
    G. 12
    H. 24
    J. 32
    K. 64

THIS IS THE END OF THE TEST. IF TIME REMAINS, YOU MAY CHECK YOUR ANSWERS TO PART 1 AND PART 2. BE SURE THAT THERE ARE NO STRAY MARKS, PARTIALLY FILLED ANSWER CIRCLES, OR INCOMPLETE ERASURES ON YOUR ANSWER SHEET. ■

PRACTICE TEST ANSWERS

VERBAL

Paragraph 1
   QSURT
Paragraph 2
   SQTRU
Paragraph 3
   SRUQT
Paragraph 4
   RQUTS
Paragraph 5
   UQRST

41. D
42. K
43. B
44. J
45. E
46. K
47. A
48. H
49. D
50. G

11. A
12. J
13. B
14. J
15. A
16. H
17. B
18. K
19. C
20. H
21. E
22. G
23. D
24. F
25. C
26. G
27. C
28. K
29. E
30. G
31. C
32. F
33. A
34. H
35. B
36. H
37. E
38. F
39. B
40. F

MATH

51. B
52. J
53. D
54. F
55. C
56. F
57. D
58. K
59. B
60. K
61. D
62. G
63. A
64. H
65. C
66. G
67. A
68. J
69. E
70. K
71. B
72. K
73. C
74. G
75. D
76. J
77. C
78. G
79. D
80. J
81. B
82. H
83. A
84. J
85. D
86. G
87. E
88. F
89. D
90. H

91. D
92. K
93. D
94. J
95. A
96. G
97. B
98. H
99. C
100. H

8

Practice Test
Explanations

VERBAL

Paragraph 1

Insects do not have spoken communications, but they have other forms of communication that are equally effective.

_____ Q. Different insects use different methods of communication.

_____ R. Ants, on the other hand, leave behind specific scent trails to mark paths to food and danger.

_____ S. Ants and bees, for example, are able to share large amounts of complex information without talking in two completely different, silent ways.

_____ T. If after these two examples it seems strange that insects can communicate, just imagine how we must seem to them.

_____ U. Bees do this by dancing out complex patterns that tell other bees where they can find food or water.

Q mentions "methods of communication" referring to "forms of communication" in the opening sentence, so it goes first. Also, in Q, "different insects" introduces "ants and bees," so Q is before S and T. S introduces "Ants and bees," so it goes before R, T, and U. R says "Ants, on the other hand," so it comes after U, which says "Bees do this by . . . ," T refers back to ants and bees with the phrase ". . . after these two examples . . ." so it must be last. So our order is QSURT.

VERBAL

QUESTIONS	EXPLANATIONS

Paragraph 2

Most people believe that when Christopher Columbus landed in America, in 1492, he was the first European to do so.

_____ Q. Recent archaeological evidence has supported alternate theories.

_____ R. When these remains were examined, the settlement was found to have been occupied in about 1000 A.D.

_____ S. However, as the twentieth century has progressed, that belief has been challenged.

_____ T. For instance, in 1963, scientists uncovered the remains of a Viking settlement on the northern tip of Newfoundland.

_____ U. Therefore, despite popular belief, the Vikings were colonizing the new world long before Christopher Columbus arrived.

S mentions "that belief" referring to "most people believe" in the opening sentence, so it goes first. Q says the belief was challenged by "archaeological evidence." The evidence is described in T, so S is before T. R mentions "these remains" so T is before R. U has a conclusion word at the beginning so it's last. Our order is SQTRU.

VERBAL

Paragraph 3

The American anole, a small desert lizard, is a pretender among pretenders.

_____ **Q.** For example, when an anole sits on a plant during a warm, dry, summer day its color is a bright, emerald green.

_____ **R.** Sometimes mistaken for a chameleon, it does not change color to match its surroundings, as real chameleons do.

_____ **S.** Often thought to be just like other lizards, this desert lizard actually has its own special characteristics.

_____ **T.** But when it is uncovered among dead leaves in the wintertime it appears a dark brown.

_____ **U.** Unlike the chameleon, the anole only changes color in response to temperature.

S refers to this "small desert lizards" mentioned in the opening sentence, so it goes first. R introduces changing color, and U expands on it , so R is before U. U introduces "temperature," and Q's "warm" and T's "wintertime" refer to it, so U is before Q and T. T starts with "but" in order to transition from Q, so Q is before T. Our order is SRUQT.

VERBAL

Paragraph 4

When most people think of spiders, they think of the webs that spiders weave.

_____ **Q.** However, even though the spider webs take a beautiful form, they also serve a deadly function.

_____ **R.** At first glance, spider webs appear intricate and beautifully crafted.

_____ **S.** One example is the wolf spider, which wanders its territory in search of prey.

_____ **T.** However, not all spiders spin these delicate and dangerous webs; some have more direct methods.

_____ **U.** For most spiders, it is their primary means of trapping the insects that make up their diet.

R introduces beauty and Q refers to it, so R is before Q. Q introduces "deadly function" and U expands on it with "trapping the insects," so Q is before U. U starts off with "For most spiders" and T responds with "However, not all . . ." so U is before T. T says "some have more direct methods," and S gives us an example of one, so T is before S. Our order is RQUTS.

VERBAL

Paragraph 5

Even though music seems to be a part of every human society, why people respond to it is a mystery.

_____ Q. One answer might be that our aptitude for music is related to our aptitude for language, but music is not just language in another form.

_____ R. When one composer suffered difficulty in communicating after he had a stroke on the left side of the brain (the side associated with language) he was still able to write beautiful compositions.

_____ S. On the other hand, when another composer experienced damage to the right side of his brain, he was still able to speak well, but lost much of his interest in music.

_____ T. This would seem to hint that there is actually an area in our brains that is responsible for our musicality.

_____ U. Why do most people throughout the world, people of every religion and culture, play and enjoy music?

U poses the question that is answered by Q, R, and S, and T talks about brains, so U must be our first sentence. Q starts the answering ("One answer") so it comes after U. R precedes S because it introduces the example involving the "left side" and S continues with "On the other hand . . . right side . . . ." T starts off with "This" which refers to the composer example in R and S, so it comes last. Our order is UQRST.

VERBAL

11. Four friends go skydiving. Jane jumps after Fred. Tim jumps first. Mary jumps before Jane, but after Fred.

In what order did they leave the plane?

A. Tim, Fred, Mary, Jane
B. Tim, Fred, Jane, Mary
C. Fred, Mary, Jane, Tim
D. Mary, Jane, Tim, Fred
E. Cannot be determined from the information given.

11. Tim is first. Jane is after Fred and Mary is between them. So it's Tim, Fred, Mary, Jane, answer (A).

12. Last Saturday, Mark spent most of the day watching television. He watched three cartoons, two football games, and one movie. After watching television, he ate dinner with his family.

According to the information given, which statement **must** be true?

F. Mark's family watched television with him.
G. Mark enjoyed the cartoons more than the football games.
H. The movie was longer than any of the other programs Mark watched.
J. Mark watched a greater number of cartoons than football games.
K. Mark started watching television before ten in the morning.

12. (F) We don't know this.
(G) We don't know this.
(H) We don't know this.
(J) Yes, this is true—the question states he watched three cartoons and two football games.
(K) We don't know this.

VERBAL

13. A dog hears higher sounds than a human does. A cat can see better in dim light than a human normally can. A shark can pick up electric signals that humans cannot sense.

Based on the information above, which of the following is a valid conclusion?

A. All animals have sensory abilities superior to humans' sensory abilities.

B. Some animals have sensory abilities that are different from humans' sensory abilities.

C. Dogs have better hearing than cats.

D. Scientists should not be surprised to find that all of a cat's senses are stronger than a dog's senses.

E. Humans do not have sensory abilities that are superior to any animal's sensory abilities.

14. At a picnic there are three boys, Maurice, Bill, and Charles, and three girls, Kysha, Leigh and Francesca. There are three pairs of brothers and sisters. Maurice is not related to Francesca. Bill is Kysha's brother.

Of the following, which is the correct pairing of brothers and sisters?

F. Maurice and Kysha, Bill and Leigh, Charles and Francesca

G. Maurice and Francesca, Bill and Kysha, Charles and Leigh

H. Maurice and Leigh, Bill and Francesca, Charles and Kysha

J. Maurice and Leigh, Bill and Kysha, Charles and Francesca

K. Maurice and Kysha, Bill and Francesca, Charles and Leigh

---

13. (A) Goes too far; we don't know about *all* animals.

(B) We know this is true from what was stated—this is the correct answer.

(C) We don't know this.

(D) This information does not imply that cats have superior senses to dogs.

(E) This statement is in no way substantiated by the information.

14. M and F aren't related, B and K are. So M has to be with L and F has to be with C. So the answer is (J).

VERBAL

QUESTIONS	EXPLANATIONS

15. In the code below, each letter stands for one of two words in a pair. The letters are not necessarily in the same order as the words. Each letter always represents the same word.

L G means "beach ball"
C L means "ball point"
C R means "point blank"
N R means "blank slate"
N P means "slate blue"
P S means "blue beard"

How would you write "blue beach" in this code?

A. P G
B. S L
C. L P
D. C S
E. N S

15. "Blue" is in the last two, which both have P, so P is "blue." Knowing this, you could eliminate all of the choices except A, because A is the only choice that contains the letter P. "Ball" is in the first two, which have L in common, so G in the first one must mean "beach." Giving us PG, answer (A).

16. Brenda notices that the neighbor's dog, Sparky, is barking. She concludes that it must now be 7 P.M.

Without any other information, which of the following statements must be true in order for Brenda's conclusion to be valid?

F. Sparky usually barks at 7 P.M.
G. There has been no barking for several days.
H. The only time Sparky barks is at 7 P.M.
J. The other dogs in the neighborhood are not barking.
K. It has been almost twenty-four hours since Brenda has last heard Sparky bark.

16. (F) doesn't go far enough to allow us to be sure it is *definitely* 7 P.M.
(G) Doesn't tell us anything about the time.
(H) This *does* tell us it has to be 7 P.M. if Sparky's barking. This is the correct answer.
(J) There is no reference to the other dogs in the neighborhood.
(K) This doesn't tell us what time it is now, Sparky could have barked at 3 P.M. to begin with.

VERBAL

17. Who is in seat number 5?

  A. Andrea
  B. Bob
  C. Edward
  D. Danielle
  E. Cannot be determined from the information given.

18. Who is in seat number 1?

  F. Danielle
  G. Christopher
  H. Edward
  J. Andrea
  K. Cannot be determined from the information given.

19. If a = 2, b = 3, c = 4, . . . , z = 27, what combination of letters would spell "Batman"?

  A. 2, 3, 14, 15, 19, 2
  B. 1, 2, 13, 1, 1, 18
  C. 3, 2, 21, 14, 2, 15
  D. 3, 2, 19, 2, 14, 15
  E. 2, 1, 18, 1, 13, 14

---

17 & 18. C is in 2, with A next to him in 1 or 3

```
1  2  3  4  5
   C  A
   A  C
```

B can't sit next to C or E. and A can't sit next to B, so

```
1  2  3  4  5
E  C  A  D  B  or
A  C  E  D  B
```

So the answer to question 17 is (B) and the answer to question 18 is (K).

19. b = 3 so we're down to answer choice (C) or (D) right away. Since the fifth letter in Batman is an A, 2 should be in the second to last spot. So our answer is (C).

VERBAL

20. All violinists who practice often and play many concerts will become world-famous. Victoria practices her violin often. Therefore, Victoria will become world-famous.

Which of the following uses reasoning that is most like the reasoning used in the paragraph above?

F. All bananas that are put in the refrigerator will turn black. This banana has been placed in the refrigerator. Therefore, this banana will turn black.

G. All sports are fun. Baseball is a sport. Therefore, baseball is fun.

H. All cakes that use the proper ingredients and are baked properly will taste delicious. This cake includes the proper ingredients. Therefore, this cake will be delicious.

J. All schools have classrooms and desks. This building has classrooms and desks. Therefore, this building is a school.

K. All fish live in water. Sharks are a type of fish. Therefore, sharks live in water.

21. Which of the following best tells what the passage is about?

A. a proof of the origin of the universe

B. an explanation of how scientists derived the age of the universe

C. a consideration of one major use of static

D. a proof of the existence of galaxies other than our own

E. a discussion of evidence for one theory of the origin of the universe

22. In order to support the big bang theory, the author mentions which of the following?

F. the results of Galileo's research

G. the discovery of low-level radiation

H. the presence of lead in the initial fireball

J. the exact temperature of the initial fireball

K. the names of scientists who performed the studies

20. The original paragraph can be summarized as: If you practice often and play many concerts you will be famous, or simply put, X and Y lead to Z. So though (F) seems like it matches, it doesn't have an X and Y part, just an X. (H) is the best match because we have "use the proper ingredients," which is X *and* "baked properly" which is Y, and these lead to Z, which is that the cake "will be delicious."

21. (E) best sums up what the passage is about. The phrase "A proof" in choice (A), though similar, is too extreme. (B) cannot be the answer because the age of the universe was not derived, and (C) cannot be the answer because static is not the main theme of the passage. As for (D), once again, "a proof" is too extreme.

22. (G) is the answer; it is the second piece of evidence given to support the big bang theory, and can be found in lines 44–45.

VERBAL

23. The discussion in lines 3–12 of the change in temperature implies that

   A. gradually, the Earth moved into a period known today as an ice age.

   B. nuclei have always been present.

   C. elementary particles are never found under extreme temperatures.

   D. nuclei did not exist under the extreme heat of the initial explosion.

   E. scientists will never know at what point nuclei began to be formed.

23. Lines 10–12 are paraphrased in answer (D). At this point in the passage, it is stated that nuclei formed as the universe cooled significantly.

24. The discussion of the cosmological principle suggests that

   F. scientists sometimes have to base their theories on other theories.

   G. scientists will never be able to concretely prove the big bang theory.

   H. we cannot make direct observations of the characteristics of the universe.

   J. the big bang started in Detroit, Michigan.

   K. scientists cannot base their theories on fact.

24. The first seven lines of paragraph two lead to answer (F).

25. In what way is measurement of the speed of light useful for scientists researching the big bang theory?

   A. Scientists can measure the speed and force of the explosion.

   B. The light distorts the images the scientists are observing.

   C. Knowing the speed of light in part provides scientists with knowledge about the universe as it once was.

   D. Scientists are able to observe the explosion as it happened.

   E. The light from the explosion has allowed scientists to make other observations in the night sky.

25. Lines 30–36 lead to answer (C).

QUESTIONS	EXPLANATIONS
26. According to the final paragraph, what is one characteristic of the static that caused scientists to associate it with the big bang?	26. Lines 40–42 lead to answer (G). The fact that the static does not originate from one place leads us to conclude that it is the remains of the original fireball.

26. (continued)

   F. The radiation was created as the universe cooled.

   G. The low-level static does not seem to be coming from one specific place.

   H. The initial fireball was comprised mostly of static.

   J. The initial explosion was equivalent in magnitude to a nuclear explosion.

   K. The low-level static was caused by a constant source of heat, over a long period of time.

27. Which of the following best tells what this passage is about?

   A. a comparison of the opossum and the kangaroo

   B. the competition between marsupials and dinosaurs

   C. the evolutionary background of kangaroos

   D. how kangaroos are not really mammals

   E. the importance of fossils in research

27. This passage starts by describing kangaroos, goes on to say that marsupials are a primitive form of mammal, then concludes, saying that kangaroos have evolved over time. Choice (C) is the best answer.

28. The author of the passage most likely agrees with which of the following statements?

   F. Opossums are smarter than kangaroos.

   G. Dinosaurs ate kangaroo meat.

   H. Kangaroos were once extinct.

   J. Kangaroos are not real mammals.

   K. Kangaroos are interesting animals.

28. In lines 1–3 of this passage, the author states that kangaroos are fascinating creatures. Fascinating is similar to interesting. Choose (K).

29. The author of the passage is most likely

   A. a hunter.

   B. a business man.

   C. a cowboy.

   D. an Australian.

   E. a scientist.

29. The second half of the first paragraph would lead us to answer (E). The author is clearly familiar with many different species of kangaroo, so perhaps he is a zoologist, a scientist who studies animals.

VERBAL

QUESTIONS	EXPLANATIONS

30. The author most likely quotes the exact size ranges in lines 15–17 in order to

   F. shock the reader.
   G. demonstrate one way in which different species of kangaroos vary greatly.
   H. contradict earlier research.
   J. prove that not all kangaroos are important.
   K. provide evidence that kangaroos have evolved in a variety of ways.

30. Lines 12–15 lead us to answer (G). These lines basically say that the different species of kangaroos vary greatly in size, color, habitat, and social behavior. (Species are basically different groups of the same animal—they're distinguished by characteristics like the ones listed.)

31. The phrase "living fossil" in line 38 refers to which of the following?

   A. a dinosaur
   B. a kangaroo
   C. an opossum
   D. an Australian marsupial
   E. a fossil of a marsupial

31. Lines 35–36 lead us to answer (C). The opossum is referred to as the living fossil, while the Australian marsupials are specifically said to *not* be living fossils.

32. What does the passage imply about the kangaroo's development?

   F. The kangaroo has adapted to its surroundings more than some other marsupials.
   G. The kangaroo had a development almost identical to that of the opossum.
   H. The kangaroo is similar to a dinosaur.
   J. The kangaroos' native habitat is North America.
   K. Kangaroos look exactly as they looked one million years ago.

32. Lines 40–43 lead us to answer (F). In line 38, it is said that opossums are living fossils, which implies that they have not evolved—in contrast, it is said that the Australian marsupials *have* evolved.

33. Which of the following best tells what this passage is about?

   A. a description of an early culture
   B. a demonstration of how ships are built
   C. a proof of the origin of the settlers of Crete
   D. a study of the advantages of a trade-oriented economy
   E. an examination of the relationship between geography and culture

33. If you wrote a one-line summary of this passage, you might have written something like: "life in ancient Crete"—this would lead you to choose (A), which is correct.

VERBAL

34. According to the passage, all of the following statements about Crete are true **except**:

  F. The land was not suitable for the development of an agricultural economy.

  G. The location of the island helped settlers to make a good living by trade.

  H. The island is surrounded by a border of jagged cliffs.

  J. The island provided a large supply of timber.

  K. People enjoyed watching bullfights.

34. Lines 4–8 tell us that (F) is true, lines 5–9 eliminate (G), lines 25–26 rule out (J), and lines 37–40 show that (K) is true, so (H) must be the answer that's not true. Though jagged mountains are mentioned (line 6), they are not a border surrounding the island.

35. According to the passage, the people of Crete were known as skilled builders because

  A. they dressed well.

  B. they designed a keel that was very advantageous in sea warfare.

  C. the population had no leisure time.

  D. the palace of Minos was a big building.

  E. the histories of other civilizations document the skills of the Cretans.

35. Lines 26–36 lead us to (B). These lines say that Cretan ships were carefully designed and expertly constructed, and also mention that several aspects of the Cretan ships made them superior war vessels.

36. According to the passage, which of the following describes the most important characteristic of the civilization of Crete?

  F. It was the first to develop bullfighting as a sport.

  G. It was a middle-class society.

  H. It was the first to start an economy based on trade and seafaring.

  J. It was preoccupied with war.

  K. It was unable to develop farming skills.

36. The first paragraph leads us to (H). The other answer choices may or may not be true (except G, which is stated in the passage, but which is not the most important characteristic of Crete).

37. According to the passage, the function of "keels covered in bronze" was

  A. to show religious devotions.

  B. to replace wood in building ships.

  C. to improve the land for farming.

  D. to support local merchants.

  E. to ram enemy ships.

37. Lines 33-34 show us that (E) is correct.

VERBAL

QUESTIONS	EXPLANATIONS

38. The final sentence of the passage suggests that

F. modern Cretans' reliance on trade is due as much to necessity as to ingenuity.
G. modern Cretans do not rely on trade to the extent that ancient Cretans did.
H. modern Cretans rely on trade only to sell manufactured goods.
J. modern Cretans deeply respect the tradition and history of maritime trade.
K. modern Cretans' trading patterns are unreliable.

38. The answer is (F). This answer is based on the fact that in the first sentence, the author states that travelers had to cross sixty miles of open water to reach Crete.

39. Which of the following best tells what this passage is about?

A. It sets forth a new definition of artistic greatness.
B. It explains the value of the music of John Philip Sousa.
C. It emphasizes the importance of band music.
D. It proves that Sousa was one of the greatest musicians of all time.
E. It shows that Sousa was more talented than Beethoven.

39. If your summary of the passage went like this: "John Philip Sousa's music—simple, practical, patriotic," you could easily choose the correct answer, (B).

40. The author would be most likely to use which of the following terms in describing the music of John Philip Sousa?

F. memorable
G. peaceful
H. jazzy
J. stupid
K. horrible

40. Lines 3–5 and lines 21–25 tell us that Sousa's marches are widely recognized, simple, and catchy. In other words, they are memorable. The answer is (F).

41. Sousa's work is "practical" (line 8) in the sense that it is

A. often imitated by classical musicians.
B. easy to forget.
C. easily learned by children.
D. actually used for military marching.
E. never actually played.

41. Lines 17–20 lead us to (D). Practical implies useful for something, and Sousa's tunes were originally written to be marched to.

VERBAL

42. The discussion of the simplicity of Sousa's marches in lines 21–27 suggests that

   F. Sousa's marches are childish.

   G. the simplicity of Sousa's marches is unnecessary.

   H. simple music is superior to complex music.

   J. Sousa did not put much thought into his work.

   K. the simplicity of Sousa's marches does not make them any less admirable.

43. What does the passage imply about the quality of Sousa's work?

   A. It is inferior to composers such as Beethoven and Wagner.

   B. Despite their simplicity, his marches merit consideration as true national classics.

   C. It is a highly complex combination of rhythm, melody, and beat.

   D. The works are good to listen to, but have little practical application.

   E. The works are hardly ever heard in today's musical world.

44. Which of the following is **not** mentioned as an aspect of Sousa's compositions?

   F. Marching bands use them very frequently.

   G. They are not equal to the complex works of Beethoven.

   H. The music is original and clearly the work of Sousa.

   J. Wagner's marches were an early influence on Sousa's works.

   K. Sousa's marches are simple.

---

42. Lines 21–27 lead us to (K). (F), (G), and (J) are all slightly derogatory (which means "saying bad things about") to Sousa's music; you can eliminate them, since the passage does nothing but praise his music. Choice (H) is simply not true.

43. Lines 40–49 lead us to (B). In fact, the entire passage pretty much backs up that statement.

44. Lines 31–35 tell us (F) is true, line 1 tells us (G) is true, lines 24–25 show that (H) and (K) are true, so (J) is the answer choice **not** mentioned and you should have chosen it.

VERBAL

45. Which of the following best tells what this passage is about?

  A. African leaders operated above the law in the past.

  B. Oppressive African governments of the late 1950s are giving way to communism.

  C. Present-day African revolutions will definitely yield to democracy and great economic wealth.

  D. Africans are experiencing a new reliance on their kin, their tribesmen, and themselves due to the changing political climate in recent years.

  E. The recent political changes in Africa have improved the potential for greater civil liberties but have also resulted in factional violence.

45. If your short summary said something like "Africa—political change, pluses and minuses" you would have chosen (E), which is correct.

46. The author's attitude toward the "dictators" in lines 14–17 is one of

  F. indifference and apathy.

  G. wholehearted approval.

  H. unbiased speculation.

  J. respect and admiration.

  K. contempt and dislike.

46. The fact that lines 16–19 says that the dictators have been "running Africa into the ground" implies that he feels contempt and dislike for them. The answer is (K).

47. The author mentions Liberia and Somalia as examples of

  A. revolutions that progressed to violence.

  B. oppressive governments that have advocated revolutions.

  C. political upheavals that have promoted Africans' self-reliance.

  D. Africans' ability to carry on daily life despite violence and revolution.

  E. governments that advocate a multi-party system.

47. Lines 28–31 lead us to (A). The author uses the dramatic term "bloodbaths" to describe the violent revolutions.

VERBAL

QUESTIONS	EXPLANATIONS

48. The author would most likely agree with all of the following statements **except**:

    F. Africans rely on their family and their tribes.

    G. Revolutions in Africa have resulted in increased civil liberties and increased violence.

    H. African revolutions are the only effective way to promote change.

    J. Revolutions in Liberia and Somalia have become particularly brutal.

    K. Despite the violence of rebel activities in Africa, the outlook for the future is better now than before any change had occurred.

48. Lines 49–57 tell us (F) is true, lines 8–15 tell us (G) is true, lines 29–31 show that (J) is true, and lines 49–57 show that (K) is true, so (H) is the one that the author wouldn't agree with.

49. The word *"paradoxically"* in line 46 is used to describe

    A. the customs and habits of the tribesmen.

    B. the power of the Big Men.

    C the balance between good and evil.

    D. the contradiction between the impact of political changes and the continuance of daily life.

    E. the impact of political upheavals in the last two years.

49. Lines 46–51 are paraphrased in answer (D). The other options do not contain any of the information in these lines.

50. According to the passage, most Africans

    F. are upset about the political upheavals.

    G. continue living their lives in the same way as before the political upheavals.

    H. think the future will be prosperous.

    J. are independent of their kin.

    K. are fighting in political revolutions.

50. Lines 46–49 lead us to (G). You might think that Choice (F) is correct, but the passage does not say this. The last paragraph of the passage, however, supports choice (G).

MATH

QUESTIONS	EXPLANATIONS

51. $\dfrac{5^2+5}{5}$

    A. 5
    B. 6
    C. 10
    D. 25
    E. 26

51. $5^2 = 25$,
25 + 5 = 30,
30 ÷ 5 = 6,
The answer is (B).

52. Express 27.8913 × 100 in scientific notation.

    F. 0.278913×10^3
    G. 0.278913×10^4
    H. 2.78913×10^2
    J. 2.78913×10^3
    K. 27.8913×10^2

52. In scientific notation, there is always one digit to the left of the decimal. That narrows it to (H) and (J). 100 is 10^2, but since we are moving the decimal once, we need 10^3 to go with 2.78913. The answer is (J).

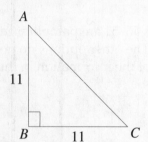

53. The above figure is an isosceles right triangle. The measure of angle C =

    A. 90
    B. 60
    C. 50
    D. 45
    E. 25

53. We have a 90-degree right angle, and since two sides are equal, the two angles opposite them are also equal. So 90 divided by 2 is 45, and the answer is (D).

54. A candy bar is advertised as costing "three for $1.00." If Jackie bought 21 candy bars at this price, how much money would she have saved if the price had been reduced to "seven for $2.00"?

    F. $1.00
    G. $1.50
    H. $2.10
    J. $3.00
    K. $7.00

54. 3 for $1 times 7 = 21 candy bars for $7, and 7 for $2 times 3 = 21 candy bars for $6, so she would have saved $1, and the answer is (F).

MATH

55. A telephone call costs $1.50 for the first three minutes, and 20 cents for each additional minute. What is the cost of a nine-minute call?

A. $1.70
B. $2.20
C. $2.70
D. $3.30
E. $4.50

55. $1.50 (for the first three minutes) + (6 minutes at 20 cents each) = 6 × 20 = 120 cents + 150 cents = $2.70. The answer is (C).

56. If $q + r + s = 117$, and $q = s = 4r$, then $r =$

F. 13
G. 18
H. 30
J. 42
K. 54

56. Since $q = s = 4r$, substitute $4r$ into $q + r + s = 117$, making it $4r + r + 4r = 117$, so $9r = 117$, and 117 divided by 9 = 13. The answer is (F).

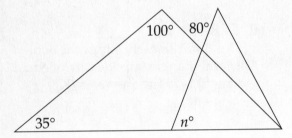

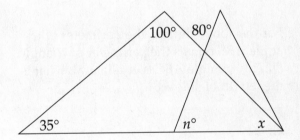

57. In the figure above, what is the value of n?

A. 25
B. 35
C. 45
D. 55
E. 80

57. Because two straight lines cross, forming an 80° angle, we know that the opposite angle is also 80°. In the large triangle, we know that $100 + 35 + x = 180$, so $x = 45$. In the small triangle, so $80 + 45 + n = 180$, and $n = 55$. The answer is (D).

58. If the sum of two numbers is 29 and their difference is 7, what is the larger of the two numbers?

F. −18
G. −11
H. 11
J. 12
K. 18

58. Backsolve—(H) and (J) are too small, so the answer is (K).

MATH

59. Over a five-week period, Tanya sold a total of 90 subscriptions. If she sold 22, 15, 20, and 18 subscriptions in the first four weeks respectively, what was the median number of magazines she sold?

 A. 15
 B. 18
 C. 20
 D. 22
 E. 25

59. She sold the 90, minus the ones we know, leaves us with 15 for the fifth week. Put the five numbers in order
 15, 15, 18, 20, 22
 So 18 is in the middle; it is the median. The answer is (B).

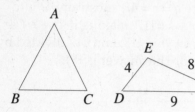

60. For the above figures, the perimeter of triangle *ABC* equals the perimeter of triangle *DEF*. If triangle *ABC* is equilateral, what is the length of side *AB*?

 F. 21
 G. 14
 H. 10
 J. 8
 K. 7

60. $4 + 8 + 9 = 21$
 $21 \div 3 = 7$, so each side of the equilateral triangle (all sides are of equal length) is 7. The answer is (K).

61. If $x = -2$ and $y = 4$ then $x^2y + \dfrac{y}{x} =$

 A. −18
 B. −14
 C. 12
 D. 14
 E. 18

61. $(-2)^2$ is 4, so $x^2y = 4 \times 4 = 16$

 and $\dfrac{4}{-2} = -2$. So $16 + -2 = 14$, and the answer is (D).

62. Eric has $3.50. Of this amount, he owes his mother 14%, and his sister 76%. How much money will Eric have left after he pays his debts?

 F. $0.10
 G. $0.35
 H. $0.70
 J. $0.72
 K. $0.84

62. $14\% + 76\% = 90\%$, so 10% is left. 10% of $3.50 is .35. The answer is (G).

MATH

63. What is the sum of all the distinct prime factors of 48?

    A. 5
    B. 6
    C. 11
    D. 36
    E. 75

63. Factors of 48: 1 and 48
                  2 and 24
                  3 and 16
                  4 and 12
                  6 and 8
Of these only 2 and 3 are prime.
$2 + 3 = 5$. The answer is (A).

64. Let # be defined by the equation $a \# b = ab + a + b$ for all numbers a and b.

    $2 \# 5 =$

    F. 7
    G. 10
    H. 17
    J. 20
    K. 32

64. Using the equation defined, 2#5 becomes $2(5) + 2 + 5$ which equals 17. The answer is (H).

65. If $n \geq 1$, then
$1^n + 1^{n+1} + 1^{n+2} + 1^{n+3} + 1^{n+4} + 1^{n+5} =$

    A. 72
    B. 15
    C. 6
    D. 5
    E. Cannot be determined from the information given.

65. 1 raised to any power is just 1. So, $1 + 1 + 1 + 1 + 1 + 1 = 6$. The answer is (C).

66. What is the decimal representation of $1,000 + 1 + \dfrac{1}{1000}$?

    F. 1,001.01
    G. 1,001.001
    H. 1,000.101
    J. 1,000.1001
    K. 1,001.0001

66. $\dfrac{1}{1000} = .001$, so

$1000 + 1 + \dfrac{1}{1000} = 1001.001$.

The answer is (G).

67. A car dealer sells b blue cars and r red cars in one day. Which of the following equations represents the statement, "The number of blue cars sold is three times the number of red cars sold"?

    A. $3r = b$
    B. $3b = r$
    C. $b + 3 = r$
    D. $b = r + 3$
    E. $3b = 3r$

67. Plug in a number for blue cars, say 15. That's 3 times 5. So r would equal 5. Which answer choice turns out to be 15 on both sides? (A).

MATH

68. $\dfrac{(0.25 + 0.25 + 0.25 + 0.25)}{4} =$

    F. 1.00
    G. 0.75
    H. 0.50
    J. 0.25
    K. 0.125

68. The top equals 1, and $\dfrac{1}{4} = .25$. The answer is (J).

69. If $5q = 3r = 30$, then $qr =$

    A. 18
    B. 32
    C. 40
    D. 50
    E. 60

69. $5q = 30$, so $q = 5$. $3r = 30$, so $r = 10$. $6 \times 10 = 60$. The answer is (E).

70. The following are coordinates of points in the xy-plane. Which of these points is nearest the origin?

    F. $(-1, -1)$

    G. $(\frac{1}{2}, \frac{1}{2})$

    H. $(\frac{1}{2}, -\frac{1}{2})$

    J. $(0, -1)$

    K. $(0, \frac{1}{2})$

70. Draw a coordinate plane and plot the points. (K) is the closest to the origin. You could also look at the numbers—those closest to 0 will be closest to the origin.

71. If 100 grams is half the mass of one object and twice the mass of another, the mass of the heavier object is how many grams more than the mass of the lighter object?

    A. 200
    B. 150
    C. 100
    D. 75
    E. 50

71. 100 grams is half 200 and twice 50. The difference between these two numbers is 150, and the answer is (B).

MATH

72. $\dfrac{2}{4} \times \dfrac{3}{6} \times \dfrac{4}{8} \times \dfrac{5}{10} =$

   F.   1

   G. $\dfrac{1}{2}$

   H. $\dfrac{1}{4}$

   J. $\dfrac{1}{8}$

   K. $\dfrac{1}{16}$

72. All four fractions reduce to $\dfrac{1}{2}$, and $\dfrac{1}{2} \times \dfrac{1}{2} \times \dfrac{1}{2} \times \dfrac{1}{2} = \dfrac{1}{16}$, the answer is (K).

TEMPERATURE IN CITY X ON DEC. 6	
6 a.m.	10° below zero
8 a.m.	2° below zero
10 a.m.	15° above zero

73. What is the average (arithmetic mean) of the temperatures shown on the table above?

   A.   5° above zero
   B.   3° above zero
   C.   1° above zero
   D.   1° below zero
   E.   2° above zero

73. $-10 + -2 + 15 = 3$, $3 \div 3 = 1$. The answer is (C).

74. Line segment RT measures 12. Segment ST is $\dfrac{1}{6}$ of RT. What is the ratio of segment ST to segment RS?

   F. $\dfrac{1}{6}$

   G. $\dfrac{1}{5}$

   H. $\dfrac{1}{3}$

   J. $\dfrac{5}{6}$

   K.   5

74. $\dfrac{1}{6}$ of 12 = 2, so ST is 2 and that leaves 10 for RS. $\dfrac{2}{10} = \dfrac{1}{5}$, answer (G).

MATH

75. If set Q contains all even integers from 4 to 36 inclusive, and set Z contains all multiples of 3, how many integers are common to both sets?

A. 3
B. 4
C. 5
D. 6
E. 7

75. The common integers are 6, 12, 18, 24, 30, 36, which totals 6 common integers. The answer is (D).

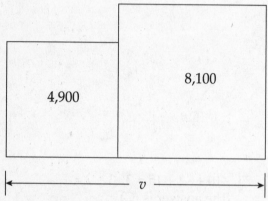

76. The above figure is composed of two squares with areas as shown. What is the value of *v*?

F. 70
G. 90
H. 140
J. 160
K. 180

76. Since these are both squares, we know that their areas are equal to the squares of their sides. This means that the lengths of sides in the left square = $\sqrt{4,900}$, or 70, and the right square = $\sqrt{8,100}$ = 90. 90 + 70 = 160. The answer is (J).

77. At 4 P.M., a 6-foot-tall man cast a shadow 10 feet long. At the same hour, how long would the shadow of a 15-foot-tall lamp post have been?

A. 9
B. 21
C. 25
D. 27
E. 30

77. Set up a proportion: $\dfrac{6}{10} = \dfrac{15}{x}$

Cross multiply; $6x = 150$, $x = 25$. The answer is (C).

MATH

QUESTIONS	EXPLANATIONS

78. What integer satisfies the following equations, $x^2 \leq x$ and $x \leq 0$?

  F. 1
  G. 0
  H. −1
  J. An infinite amount.
  K. Cannot be determined from the information given.

78. Backsolve. 0 works, 1 and −1 don't, so the answer is (G).

79. The ratio of apples to bananas at a fruit stand is 5 to 4. The ratio of cherries to bananas is 2 to 5. What is the ratio of apples to cherries?

  A. 5:5
  B. 5:2
  C. 4:5
  D. 25:8
  E. Cannot be determined from the information given.

79. A B C Use 20 as the number for y because both 4 and 5 go into it evenly. This means you have to multiply the top row by 5, which gives you 25 for A. You have to multiply the bottom row by 4, which gives you 8 for C. So the answer to the question is 25:8; (D).

      5 : 4
        5 : 2
      25:20: 8

80. On Tuesday, $\frac{2}{3}$ of a large block of ice melted. On Wednesday, $\frac{1}{2}$ of the remaining ice melted. If the block of ice then weighed 60 pounds, how much did it weigh, in pounds, at the beginning of the day on Tuesday?

  F. 540
  G. 480
  H. 450
  J. 360
  K. 180

80. Backsolve, starting with (H). $450 \times \frac{1}{3}$ (the amount of ice remaining after $\frac{2}{3}$ of it has melted) = 150, $150 \times \frac{1}{2} = 75$; this is too big.

Try (J). $360 \times \frac{1}{3} = 120$, $120 \times \frac{1}{2} = 60$.

81. What is the **least** integer greater than −3.7?

  A. −4
  B. −3
  C. 0
  D. 1
  E. 4

81. The smallest, or least integer bigger than −3.7, is −3, so the answer is (B).

MATH

82. If 20% of the science students at Central High study only physics, 25% study only chemistry and the rest study only biology, what is *the smallest number* of science students who could be studying biology?

    F. 4
    G. 9
    H. 11
    J. 15
    K. 20

82. Backsolve—start with the smallest, since that's what's being asked for. Could 4 be 55% of the students? No. Could 9 be 55% of the students? No. Could 11 be 55% of the students? Yes, the answer is (H).

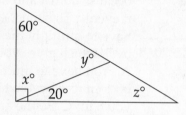

83. In the above triangle, what is the value of z, in terms of x?

    A. $100 - x$

    B. $80 - x$

    C. $x - 40$

    D. $x + 20$

    E. $\dfrac{x}{2}$

83. We know that $20 + x$ must equal 90, so $x = 70$. $70 + 60 + y = 180$, so $y = 50$. $y +$ the adjacent angle must equal 180, so that angle $= 130$. $20 + 130 + z = 180$, so $z = 30$. Choice (A) is correct, since $100 - x$ (which is 70) $= 30$.

84. If $x + 2y = 6$, and $z = 7$, what is the value of $2x + 4y + z$?

    F. 6
    G. 12
    H. 15
    J. 19
    K. 25

84. If $x + 2y = 6$, double it and you get $2x + 4y = 12$. Add z (which is 7) and you get 19; the answer is (J).

85. $(2a^3b^2t^5)^3 =$

    A. $2a^6b^8t^8$
    B. $6a^6b^5t^8$
    C. $6a^6b^4t^{10}$
    D. $8a^9b^6t^{15}$
    E. $8a^{27}b^8t^{125}$

85. Raise each of the elements to the third: 2 becomes 8, a^3 becomes a^9, b^2 becomes b^6, and t^5 becomes t^{15}, so the answer is (D).

MATH

QUESTIONS	EXPLANATIONS

86. A jogger completes one lap around a circular lake with radius = r. Another jogger completes one lap around a lake with a radius = $r + 4$. How much further does the second jogger run?

    F. 8

    G. 8π

    H. $8\pi + r$

    J. 16

    K. 16π

86. Plug in—lets say the radius is 2. So the first circumference is 4π since the circumference equation is $c = 2\pi r$. The second radius is $2\pi r(r+4) = 2\pi r + 8\pi$, and the difference is 8π, which is answer (G).

87. $\left(\dfrac{1}{2} + \dfrac{2}{5}\right) = \dfrac{9}{10}$

    A. $5\dfrac{2}{3}$

    B. 5.31

    C. 5.00

    D. $4\dfrac{2}{3}$

    E. 4.31

87. $\left(\dfrac{1}{2} + \dfrac{2}{5}\right) = \dfrac{9}{10}$,

$\dfrac{9}{10} = .9$,

$.9^2 = .81$,

$3.5 + .81 = 4.31$

The answer is (E).

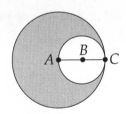

88. A circle with center B is inscribed in a circle with center A such that AC is both the diameter and the radius, respectively, of the two circles. If $BC = 3$, what is the area of the shaded region?

    F. 27π

    G. 21π

    H. 18π

    J. 9π

    K. 3π

88. The radius of the big circle is 6, so the area is πr^2 or 36π. The radius of the small circle is 3, so the area is $\pi \times 3^2 = 9\pi$, and $36\pi - 9\pi = 27\pi$; the answer is (F).

MATH

QUESTIONS	EXPLANATIONS

89. If $\dfrac{a}{b} < \dfrac{b}{a}$, $a^2 = 2a$ and $ab = 18$, what is the value of b?

A. 2
B. 3
C. 6
D. 9
E. 18

89. Answer (D). Try plugging in, with $b = 6$. So $a = 3$, does $(3)^2 = (2)(3)$? No. Try $b = 9$, and $a = 2$. Does $(2)^2 = 2(2)$?

Yes. Is $\dfrac{2}{9} < \dfrac{9}{2}$? Yes. The answer is (D).

90. A compact disc is placed in a player that randomly selects and plays songs from the disc. The compact disc contains 3 ballads, 4 instrumental pieces, X dance tracks, and no other pieces. If the probability that the first song played will be a ballad is $\dfrac{1}{4}$, what is the value of X?

F. 1
G. 4
H. 5
J. 9
K. 12

90. Backsolve for (H). $3 + 4 + 5 = 12$, $\dfrac{3}{12} = \dfrac{1}{4}$ so (H) is our answer. You could also notice that since there is a $\dfrac{1}{4}$ chance that the first song will be a ballad, there must be 4(3) total songs, or 12. 12 – the total number of other songs (7) = 5.

91. What is $-12 - (-10\tfrac{1}{2})$?

A. $-3\tfrac{1}{2}$

B. -3

C. $-2\tfrac{1}{2}$

D. $-1\tfrac{1}{2}$

E. $1\tfrac{1}{2}$

91. $-12 + 10\tfrac{1}{2} = -1\tfrac{1}{2}$, the answer is (D).

Remember that two negatives equal a positive.

MATH

92. Kai rides his bicycle up the hill to school and back every day. If he travels twice as fast downhill as up, and it takes 30 minutes round-trip, how far away is his school?

    F. 20 miles
    G. 18 miles
    H. 10 miles
    J. 6 miles
    K. Cannot be determined from the information given.

93. An eight-sided die with faces numbered 1 through 8 is rolled twice. What is the probability that the first roll will be 3 and the second roll will be 8 if the die can never be rolled as a 6?

    A. $\dfrac{1}{8}$

    B. $\dfrac{2}{8}$

    C. $\dfrac{2}{7}$

    D. $\dfrac{1}{49}$

    E. $\dfrac{2}{49}$

94. If, $\dfrac{3n-6}{7-4} = 11$ then $n =$

    F. 7
    G. 9
    H. 11
    J. 13
    K. 15

92. We don't know his speed, so we can't determine the distance. The answer is (K).

93. The probability is $\dfrac{1}{7}$ for 3 and $\dfrac{1}{7}$ for 8, and $\dfrac{1}{7} \times \dfrac{1}{7} = \dfrac{1}{49}$, answer (D). The reason that the probability is $\dfrac{1}{7}$ is that in the question it is stated that 6 is never rolled.

94. $\dfrac{3n-6}{7-4} = 11$ Cross multiply, so $3n - 6 = 33$, $3n = 39$, $n = 13$, and the answer is (J).

MATH

95. The weight of a barrel when empty is $\frac{1}{4}$ of the weight of the water it contains when full. If, when full, the barrel and water weigh a total of 20 pounds, what is the weight, in pounds, of the empty barrel?

    A. 4
    B. 5
    C. 15
    D. 16
    E. 80

95. Backsolve—start with (C). The barrel would be 15, so the water would be 60, 15 + 60 = 75; too big. (B) the barrel would be 5; so the water would be 20; 5 + 20 = 25; this is still too big. So the answer is (A).

96. Wesley, Denzel, and Earvin all pitched in to buy a VCR. Wesley paid twice as much as Earvin, and Earvin paid three times as much as Denzel. Together, the trio spent $350. How much did Earvin pay?

    F. $ 95
    G. $105
    H. $110
    J. $120
    K. $160

96. Backsolve, starting with (H), Earvin paid $110, Wesley paid $220, and Denzel about $36. The total is about 366; too big. Try (G), E = $105, W = $210, and D = $35, 105 + 210 + 35 = 350, so (G) is our answer.

97. If $x + y = 7$ and $x^2 + y^2 = 25$, what does $2xy$ equal?

    A. 14
    B. 24
    C. 28
    D. 36
    E. 48

97. $(x + y)^2 = 7^2$ and factored out, $x^2 + 2xy + y^2 = 49$, so $25 + 2xy = 49$, $2xy = 24$, and the answer is (B).

MATH

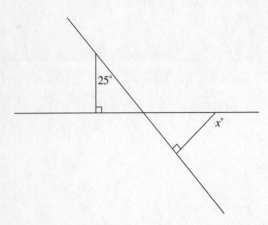

98. In the figure above, $x =$

F. 25
G. 65
H. 155
J. 160
K. 165

99. $\left(3 \times \dfrac{1}{100}\right) + \left(4 \times \dfrac{1}{10}\right) + \left(5 \times \dfrac{1}{1000}\right) + 6(1)$

A. 0.6435
B. 3.456
C. 6.435
D. 6.543
E. 64.35

98. In the upper left triangle we have a 90-degree angle and a 25-degree angle, so the third angle must be 65 degrees. The opposite angle is 65 and there is another 90-degree angle in the second triangle, so the third angle is 25, and the angle with which it makes a straight line must be 155, (H).

99. $\dfrac{3}{100} + \dfrac{4}{10} + \dfrac{5}{1000} + 6 = 6.435$, the answer is (C).

MATH

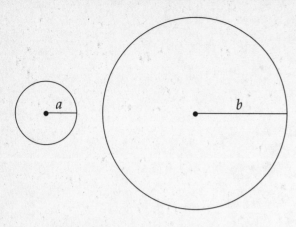

Note: Figure not drawn to scale.

100. In the figure above, two circles have radii of a and b, respectively. If $a = \frac{1}{3}b$, and the sum of the circumferences of the two circles is 64π, then what is the value of b?

    F.   8
    G. 12
    H. 24
    J.   32
    K. 64

100. Try plugging in (H) first. If $b = 24$, this means that $a = 8$, since it is $\frac{1}{3}$ of b. So the circumference formula is $c = 2\pi r$, and we need to add the two circumferences:
$2(\pi)24 + 2(\pi)8 = 64\pi$
Answer choice (H) is correct.

Completely darken bubbles with a No. 2 pencil. If you make a mistake, be sure to erase mark completely. Erase all stray marks.

YOUR NAME: _____
(Print)
       Last   First   M.I.

SIGNATURE: _____   DATE: ___/___/___

HOME ADDRESS: _____
(Print)
       Number and Street

_____
     City   State   Zip Code

PHONE NO.: _____
(Print)

Verbal Section

Paragraph 1
The first sentence is   Q R S T U
The second sentence is   Q R S T U
The third sentence is   Q R S T U
The fourth sentence is   Q R S T U
The fifth sentence is   Q R S T U

Paragraph 2
The first sentence is   Q R S T U
The second sentence is   Q R S T U
The third sentence is   Q R S T U
The fourth sentence is   Q R S T U
The fifth sentence is   Q R S T U

Paragraph 3
The first sentence is   Q R S T U
The second sentence is   Q R S T U
The third sentence is   Q R S T U
The fourth sentence is   Q R S T U
The fifth sentence is   Q R S T U

Paragraph 4
The first sentence is   Q R S T U
The second sentence is   Q R S T U
The third sentence is   Q R S T U
The fourth sentence is   Q R S T U
The fifth sentence is   Q R S T U

Paragraph 5
The first sentence is   Q R S T U
The second sentence is   Q R S T U
The third sentence is   Q R S T U
The fourth sentence is   Q R S T U
The fifth sentence is   Q R S T U

Verbal Section (continued)

11. A B C D E
12. F G H J K
13. A B C D E
14. F G H J K
15. A B C D E
16. F G H J K
17. A B C D E
18. F G H J K
19. A B C D E
20. F G H J K
21. A B C D E
22. F G H J K
23. A B C D E
24. F G H J K
25. A B C D E
26. F G H J K
27. A B C D E
28. F G H J K
29. A B C D E
30. F G H J K
31. A B C D E
32. F G H J K
33. A B C D E
34. F G H J K
35. A B C D E
36. F G H J K
37. A B C D E
38. F G H J K
39. A B C D E
40. F G H J K
41. A B C D E
42. F G H J K
43. A B C D E
44. F G H J K
45. A B C D E
46. F G H J K
47. A B C D E
48. F G H J K
49. A B C D E
50. F G H J K

Math Section

51. A B C D E
52. F G H J K
53. A B C D E
54. F G H J K
55. A B C D E
56. F G H J K
57. A B C D E
58. F G H J K
59. A B C D E
60. F G H J K
61. A B C D E
62. F G H J K
63. A B C D E
64. F G H J K
65. A B C D E
66. F G H J K
67. A B C D E
68. F G H J K
69. A B C D E
70. F G H J K
71. A B C D E
72. F G H J K
73. A B C D E
74. F G H J K
75. A B C D E
76. F G H J K
77. A B C D E
78. F G H J K
79. A B C D E
80. F G H J K
81. A B C D E
82. F G H J K
83. A B C D E
84. F G H J K
85. A B C D E
86. F G H J K
87. A B C D E
88. F G H J K
89. A B C D E
90. F G H J K
91. A B C D E
92. F G H J K
93. A B C D E
94. F G H J K
95. A B C D E
96. F G H J K
97. A B C D E
98. F G H J K
99. A B C D E
100. F G H J K

ABOUT THE AUTHOR

Jonathan Arak has been associated with The Princeton Review since 1982, when he was a student of founder and CEO John Katzman. After graduating from Oberlin College in 1988, he returned to New York and became a teacher for The Princeton Review, trained by Mr. Katzman. Since then he has prepared thousands of students for standardized tests. Accepted at Stuyvesant while attending and graduating from Hunter College High School, the author has first-hand experience with the SHSAT. Since 1993, he has put that experience to use as The Princeton Review's Master Trainer for the SHSAT, for which he has trained the new SHSAT teachers and co-written the course manual.

NOTES

NOTES

NOTES

NOTES

NOTES

NOTES

NOTES

NOTES

NOTES

If students need to know it, it's in our Roadmap Guides!